WHEN
NATURE
CALLS

WHEN NATURE CALLS

Life at a Gulf Island Cottage

ERIC NICOL

HARBOUR PUBLISHING

Published by
HARBOUR PUBLISHING
P.O. Box 219
Madeira Park, BC Canada
V0N 2H0

THE CANADA COUNCIL | LE CONSEIL DES ARTS
FOR THE ARTS | DU CANADA
SINCE 1957 | DEPUIS 1957

Edited by Michael Carroll
Printed and bound in Canada

Harbour Publishing acknowledges the financial support of the Government of Canada through the Book Publishing Industry Development Program (BPIDP) and the Canada Council for the Arts, and the Province of British Columbia through the British Columbia Arts Council, for its publishing activities.

Canadian Cataloguing in Publication Data

Nicol, Eric, 1919–
    When nature calls

    ISBN 1-55017-210-7

    1. Saturna Island (B.C.)—Humor. I. Title.
PS8527.I35W53 1999   971.1'28   C99-910893-X
PR9199.3.N5W53 1999

In the downhill of life, when I find I'm declining
May my lot no less fortunate be
Than a snug elbow-chair can afford for reclining
And a cot that o'erlooks the wide sea . . .

—John Collins, "Tomorrow"

Contents

Introduction

Driver, Follow That Dream!

The summer cottage. Luxury or necessity? Do you really *need* a summer place in the outback, or can a person survive year-round in urban condomation without getting into mind-altering drugs or politics?

To the working poor, the concept of owning a summer cottage is pure fancy. They associate the alternate, seasonal residence with the French Riviera villa owned by an Arab prince, or a Hollywood movie star, or a Canadian orthodontist. Their first priority is to get out of the rental and into a mortgage issued by a bank that has temporarily taken leave of its senses.

But I like to think that even the most impoverished denizen of public housing dreams, from time to time, or when delirious with hunger, that one day he or she will win the $6-million lottery that will make owning a summer cottage almost affordable. To believe otherwise would be somehow elitist and could limit the sales of this book.

The one class of people for whom the ideal of escaping to a summer cottage is not rhapsodic is, of course, your average teenager. To most adolescents, the prospect of being confined with their parents, miles from the nearest mall, is a preview of Hell. I must reluctantly admit that potential readership for this book mainly comprises legally sane persons over eighteen years of age. And I have been able to convince the publisher that honesty has its place.

But certainly for *younger* children (two to twelve) the idea of frolicking in a summer cottage should be irresistible. They have been read the exciting adventures in woodsy cottages of Hansel and Gretel and Little Red Riding Hood. I am confident that every small child will gain an insight into the rural charm that drew Goldilocks into the cottage of the Three Bears. Construction details (see Chapters 8 to 10) aren't unlike those that created problems for the Three Little Pigs, though wolfproof straw is now available as framing.

However, to judge by the people lined up for the ferries to cottage country, the majority of folk fleeing the city are of mature years.

The typical cottager is grey-haired. Rarely is he or she bald. Bald people lean to RVs and trailers, according to some studies I intend to make. They wear baseball caps, enjoy gambling and are highly social, travelling thousands of miles in a motor home in order to park cheek by jowl with dozens of other motor homes in an RV park. They are apt to use a cologne, something a cottager would die before doing.

Besides being an older if not wiser adult, the person who develops a craving for a summer cottage is likely to be a male. Women are the more sociable animal, not naturally drawn to isolation, snakes and ladders. For a woman, talking is the most important function of her mouth, after eating. Not like men, for whom it's spitting. A man can go for days without saying a word to anyone but a raccoon, a chainsaw or himself—a prime prerequisite for the cottager.

"To get away from the noise and pollution of the city"— that's the reason often given by a man for having a summer cottage, the place where he fires up the generator that does a number on both his eardrums and his respiratory system. But it is *his* noise and *his* pollution. To be personally responsible for our own afflictions is one of the great comforts of the summer cottage, though this is less appreciated by the wife and mother.

But there are other stimuli that prompt men to lust for a cottage. All of us should be asked, before we become too aroused by a floor plan, "What is your real motivation?" If we can't answer that question, in twenty-five words or less, then the set square should be pried from our fingers and cold water dashed in our faces until we make a coherent reply.

Here it is all too easy to rationalize. My own alleged reason for building a summer cottage was to provide my teenage children with a sanctuary from Temptation, which is rampant in a city like Vancouver whose moral standards have never been compared favourably with those of Moose Jaw, Saskatchewan. For some reason, I believed that the absence of rock bands and nightclubs on Saturna Island would be a benign sedative for young people such as my spawn.

In this I erred big-time. The cottage was a nice place to visit on a momentary basis, but they wouldn't want to stay there and pay rent.

I subsequently improved the place, by adding a stove and windows, and began to enjoy the cottage myself. Was this my subconscious intent from the start? A purely selfish enterprise? The suspicion nags, but only when I'm thinking.

Thus, in the course of creating a comfortable habitation on my property, I learned how right English biologist Julian Huxley was when he reminded us that all birds—except the cuckoo—have instinctive knowledge of how to build a nest. They don't learn it from their parents. Birds don't have to go to an avian Home Depot and chirp for help from a clerk. They are simply born with the savvy to construct not only a fully furnished home of twigs and/or mud but of a predetermined design that satisfies God's building code.

What a talent! How relatively stupid have I felt contemplating the building of *my* cottage and running around aimlessly with bits of shoot in my mouth!

If my brain hadn't got cluttered up with reasoning power based on experience—a part of their brain that birds have sensibly left undeveloped—I would know automatically how to whip together a nice, wicker, five-room nest, with my female mate doing most of the bull work.

Instead of brooding about being unfledged and clueless about home-building, the potential cottager should understand that birds are motivated solely by the need to have a place in which to lay their eggs—an urge that I and most other humans rarely experience—and to rear their young.

Well, if not as a place to give birth in, what of the summer cottage as the place to die in? It's a romantic notion: that we can escape the ghastly fate of going to black in a nursing home by building a terminal abode wired for the exit.

But it's been tried, with negative results. Michel de Montaigne, in his essay "Of Judging the Death of Others," tells the story of the Roman emperor Heliogabalus who, toward the end of a short life of debauchery, put his mind to planning a first-class luxury suicide:

- He had a high tower built, faced with gold and precious stones, and a grand staircase within that he could climb, elegantly and on cue, to throw himself off the top.

- He ordered silken cords of crimson and gold with which to strangle himself and a golden sword on which to be impaled.

- He kept a cellar of poisons, stored in vases inlaid with emerald and topaz, so that he could drink them when the Reaper beckoned.

And having lavished upon himself all these options for an opulent death, what happened? Heliogabalus was murdered by popular demand.

The moral of his story for the cottager is: build it to live in, not to die in. Forget the high tower. Skip the hara-kiri room. Don't bother to add the cellar of vintage venom. The blessings of the summer cottage are those that cost the least: the sweet, sweet air; the renewed kinship with wild critturs; the retirement of the middle finger to its proper role in a working hand.

What follows is one cottager's reflections on these rewards of the sanest of asylums.

1

Isles of the Blest

Celtic legend placed them in the Western Ocean. They were the Fortunate Isles, where the souls of mortals A-rated by the gods romped in a paradise for eternity, or at least until the property taxes went up.

For a time, the Isles of the Blest were thought to be the Canaries, or the Madeiras, but no longer. Those Atlantic Edens lost the sponsorship of Heaven when shiploads of European tourists started arriving in the all-too-solid flesh. Today, for those fortunate enough to have discovered them, the blessed are the southern Gulf Islands of British Columbia.

Truly these are islands to die for. But being deceased isn't a prerequisite for us whom the gods have smiled on as eligible.

We don't argue with those who contend that the islands of Hawaii are more favoured because of more prevalent sunshine, pineapples and lively flows of red-hot lava. But we *could* point out that for a Canadian to own a Hawaiian island is somewhat pricey, if not prohibited by US law. In contrast, people are still able to buy one of the southern Gulf Islands. It may not be a *large* island, and the purchaser may have to adjust to sharing a bare rock with 3,000 gulls, but there is relatively little crime.

Gulf Islanders are confident that God created Vancouver Island—that Belgium-size whopper of an isle—in order to protect our smaller islands from the notoriously bad temper of the Pacific Ocean. Whoever named that boisterous body of water "pacific" must have caught it in a rare good mood, or glimpsed it—like the misidentified "stout Cortez"—from a peak well inland . . . on a foggy day . . . after a liquid lunch.

What these Gulf Islands lack in lure for surfers, they compensate for with myriad salty channels, sounds, passes, bays and coves that hardly ever see a monster wave. These waters deal heavily in ripples. Instead of breakers booming upon the browbeaten shore, they engage in tidal round dances. Fiddler's Cove, on Saturna Island, hosts just such aquatic hoedowns.

Saturna, and her sister islands of the southern Strait of Georgia—Galiano, Salt Spring, Pender, Mayne—are also much obliged to Vancouver Island for intercepting that other manic form of moisture: rain. While the west coast of the big island is lashed with as much as 200 inches of rain a year, its mountains scare the peecip out of clouds so that the Gulf Islands commonly receive less than a quarter of that amount. They would never claim to be semi-arid, mind you, and attempts to grow palm trees on these islands haven't been an unqualified success.

But their islanders prefer to describe visible humidity as "heavy mist." In winter the mist sometimes settles as what at first glance looks like snow. Heavy mist up to the waist isn't totally unknown.

Much as the Mafia has its code of silence about gang mayhem, islanders take an oath to keep mum about snow. Their snowplow, like Saddam Hussein's Scud missiles, is kept hidden in a secret shed. Alpine sports are severely dealt with. Skis may be confiscated at the dock. And the islands are the only place in Canada where outdoor ice-skating is not only unknown but seen as an exotic custom of the East.

This semitropical climate serves as a magnet for cottagers. Not *all* cottagers, of course. Some cottagers are allergic to an island. When they find themselves on an island, their first, and pressing, desire is to get *off* the island. Islophobia isn't discussed in the literature of psychosis, but it may stem from a fear of being entirely surrounded by water. Bed-wetting, in childhood, likely helps to create this complex that makes a person vaguely uncomfortable, even on a large island, like Australia.

But to those of us who aren't gravely maladjusted, the island is a refuge from humanity. We view the Strait of Georgia as a God-given moat—with no drawbridge. We don't have alligators in our moat, but the killer whales fill in nicely.

Typical Gulf Islands cottagers have insular personalities. They accept being members of the human species, but don't want to be reminded. Their favourite novel is *Robinson Crusoe*, and they vote for the political party whose social conscience was lost when the ship of state foundered.

The Gulf Islander, in grudging concert with the other cottagers in the strait, is kept legally hostile to change by means of the Islands Trust, whose full name is the Islands Trust Nobody. Its mandate: to preserve this Eden from the serpent of Progress, with a forest program that excludes the Tree of Knowledge. You want apples? Try the Okanagan.

I wasn't looking for fruit when I first set eyes on Saturna Island. The southernmost of the major Gulf Islands, Saturna lies closer to the international border with the United States than her sisters, but doesn't have to like it.

This island is somewhat anvil-shaped, reflecting something of the nature of the residents. It is mostly rock. Its mountains were thrust out of the Earth by some tectonic convulsion that endowed it with an abundance of antisocial cliffs. Gale-force winds whip these ramparts with regularity, felling the pines whose rotting cadavers provide the nourishment for a new generation to dare the wind: "Try to do that again!"

My discovery of Saturna occurred in the late 1950s. Employed as a columnist by Vancouver's *Province*, I heard about this wondrous island at the office, about the beatific beaches where a person could sun in the nude, without a tongue to cluck disapproval and possibly a summons.

I was no swimmer, but the vision of paddling au naturel sounded like fun. So, as did several other journalists repulsed by reality, I journeyed to this fabled isle.

It is the most impractical destination of all the islands. It took seven hours, as I recall, for the *Lady Rose*—a barely glorified tug—to shove off from Steveston, sidle down the south arm of the Fraser River, strike out hopefully across the Strait of Georgia under the illusion that she was seaworthy, tax her rudder in the corkscrew of Active Pass, hang a haggard left down Navy Channel and at last crawl into Lyall Harbour, clutching at the wharf as if resolved never to leave it.

Saturna lived up to its billing. It was a magic island. Under the aegis of the Money family, who owned all the property that mattered, and whose earthy patriarch, Jim Money, was also the entire highways maintenance department, Saturna was, and still is, a paradise with only a few strategically placed potholes.

I promptly bought a lot on Boot Cove for $500. I later bought three more adjacent lots overlooking Boundary Pass—each 90 feet by 180 feet—for $1,000 apiece. Other *Province* writers also put their money where their hearts were, little dreaming, of course, that we were investing in realty that would, in time, go bananas. Dumb luck is better than no luck at all.

Our holy grail was to build a cottage on this island. And this most of us did. In fact, I built *two* cottages, one at each site, selling the first one when the birth of a third child required a caesarean on the concept of a one-room, double-bunk haven for a husband and wife.

So I have long had at least one cottage on Saturna as insurance against *dementia urbanus*, symptomized by the strumming of the lower lip and set off by the incessant whooping of a neighbour's security-alarm system.

For those considering taking out such a term policy, the chapters that follow are cordially addressed.

2

The Call of the Mild

What is the most important thing that a man measures in inches? On Saturna it's the annual rainfall. Average: forty inches. Compared to some parts of the west coast of nearby Vancouver Island, where five times that amount is common, this island is a Sahara. *The* desert island. To match its paucity of precip, it is necessary to travel to the Interior of British Columbia and find scenic fulfillment in sagebrush.

But it would be distorting the truth to say that Saturna is competitive with Palm Springs as a dry climate sought by wealthy wheezers. In fact, a number of the island residents—traitors whose names are known to authorities—spend their winters in Mexico. They are not snowbirds but rainducks. They fail to appreciate week after week of grey sky as moisturized sunshine. They abandon a very acceptable UV rating for the lands of mariachi and melanoma. Weak, weak, weak.

Many islanders are also in denial about having ever seen snow. They may wonder, audibly, at their vista of the chronically snowcapped mountains of the Olympic Peninsula, exclaiming at "that white stuff on top." But the cruel fact is that snow has been known to fall on Saturna. It rarely "settles," of course. "Settled" snow is measured as six feet or more. This freak never stays long. A few hours. A couple of days. A month at most. Then—*fftt!*—the prevailing semitropical climate takes care of the anomaly.

However, islanders who have witnessed the falling and fleeting presence of frozen moisture describe the transformation as "a winter wonderland." The buying of snow tires being an island taboo—an offender could be drummed out of the Saturna community club—inhabitants enjoy the once-in-a-lifetime thrill of being snowbound without having to set up camp on Mount Everest.

A few aliens exploit this phenomenon by deliberately coming to the island to show off their expensive all-terrain vehicles. Islanders regard this flouting of snow conditions as a graceless display of the will to live. They lean back and wait for the driver to learn that the ATV hasn't been built that can plumb the potholes on certain Saturna roads, heaved by aberrant frost and capable of swallowing a Leopard tank.

Here I must make an editorial aside: every paradise like Saturna should have a few roads like these, known to the residents as nemesis for any vehicle but the chariots of the gods. Not only do these killer roads provide employment for the local garage/body shop ("new suspension systems our specialty"), but they demolish any thought of immigration. A form of population control is what these roads are, and a lot more fun than the condom.

But we Saturna regulars take pride bordering on hubris in

our *essential* roads. The one-man snow removal truck has them cleared before crews in the city have got out of bed. There is absolutely no need for the cottager to maintain a sled and dog team just to enjoy Christmas on the island. Help *will* arrive. Phoning 911, in panic, is considered infra dig, very poor form, unless one's personal snow clearing has induced clear symptoms of a heart attack.

Much more than the Mainland blizzard, what puts the wind up the Saturnan is hurricane. We do not, of course, *call* it a hurricane. Hurricanes with given names—Gus, Harry, Ida—are something that happen to people in lower latitudes who probably deserve them. North of Forty-nine, we get only rather strong wind. Megabreezes, you might say. Some of these register at 100 miles per hour, but only in gusts of. A gust may last as long as four or five hours. You might not even notice it, except for the crash of large trees being blown down on your property. These trees were obviously ready to lose their verticality. Shallow-rooted, most of them, they succumbed to zephyr-enhanced gravity. Too bad they took out the hydro line.

That last blusterous effect is why candles are not entirely unknown in Saturna cottages. Some residents are climatically defensive enough to insist that they keep candles only for religious ceremonies, such as the blessing of the first dinghy to go fishing illegally. But in the absence of a synagogue or a Roman Catholic church on the island, and the small demand for candelabra on grand pianos, the laying in of candles does say something about the impact of what might—if one insisted on being verbally fastidious—be called a windstorm.

This unwonted occurrence is more than offset by the temperance of an island climate that is the joy of the truck farmer—Fords, mostly. There may not be a chicken in every pot, but there is a truck in every driveway, waiting to groan under the weight of cucumbers, carrots, all manner of other vegetables, to be borne to the farmers' market in the Community Hall, where a fortune teller will read your Tarot cards and tell you whether it is wise to lay in a lifetime supply of zucchini.

As the northernmost of the South Pacific islands, Saturna yields bounteous crops—flowers and legumes—weeks ahead of the so-called Mainland. This island is fully competitive with Victoria, the capital city on Vancouver Island, where everything matures early except the members of the legislature.

If William Wordsworth were seeking daffodils in February, Saturna would be the place to wander lonely as a cloud, after his deodorant died.

On the matter of clouds: one of my duties as a sky-watcher is to inspect clouds drifting up from the United States, driven by a Border-collie breeze. I check them out for carrying an illegal substance, such as rain. But mostly I just wave them through . . .

"Welcome to Canada, clouds! Hope you enjoy your stay . . ."

To sum up: Saturna folk look upon rain clouds as God's own sprinkler system. It keeps us green and growing, and if we find moss in our shorts, well, it's kind of mystical.

3

Art for Whose Sake?

The Gulf Islands are known for their artists and writers. These are one of the few forms of life here not threatened by civilization. There has been no need to organize an environmental group to save the old-growth potter, or the shy, nut-eating poet.

Novelists, too, abound on these enchanted isles. Few of them write bestsellers, but the island earth nurtures a bumper crop of hopes.

Why starve in a chilly garret, town-side, when you can enjoy malnutrition in such pleasant surroundings?

British Columbia's greatest artist, Emily Carr, was a child of the islands, and set the tone for succeeding waves of painters seeking to capture the soul of a cedar stump, on canvas. Rare indeed is the island beach whose sand does not bear the footprint of the crafty easel.

All of these artists—whom we may call the Group of Seven Thousand—paint nature scenes. There is no market for portraiture any more, on the islands or off. *The Blue Boy* has been replaced by *The Blue Berries*. There is no record of an island painter's having lopped off an ear and sent it to a friend, possibly because there is no courier service.

A few of the island artists have become wealthy and world-famous—Robert Bateman being such a rarity. His paintings of the wild, and especially the prices they bring, have inspired hundreds of other artists to go hunting with sketchbook and pencil, creating congestion around driftwood and other such mother lodes.

Each of the islands has its own art gallery where the visitor may buy a memento of Elysium. These art galleries display not only paintings but decorative objects constructed of beach pebbles, broken glass, clamshells, petrified wood, eagle feathers and just about any other material that cost the artist nothing to acquire.

Saturna, too, has its modest art gallery. I haven't yet browsed among its objets d'art, though not because I'm susceptible to impulse-buying. That particular impulse is one that I have always been able to control, especially when confronted with a mobile sculpture comprising pendulant fishnet floats studded with contemporary bottle caps.

In absentia, however, I fully support the art gallery as a repository of dreams for our small colony of artists. I may even buy a painting for our cottage wall as soon as the lino is paid for. I figure that one painting should do it. My wife, Mary, has identified framed pictures as preeminent dust catchers, and therefore bad for our rhinitis.

This is the main benefit I enjoy from being allergic to dust: it saves me a fortune on paintings, rugs and other furniture that has won the Golden Glove for catching dust. It would be sheer hell to have to live in the Palace of Versailles. But on the island a person breathes easily in a spartan, monkish room enhanced by a single, living seascape framed by our window: *Sunlit Chop on the Chuck*, by Creator.

Nor do I feel socially obliged to buy the novels of writers who share the island's blessings with me. Luckily we don't have many identified novelists on Saturna—in fact, none. This is odd, because other Gulf Islands—Galiano, Salt Spring, Hornby, Bowen—fairly crawl with fiction writers, so many that it isn't really safe for non-novelists to live on those islands, given the large chance they will end up as characters in a story, the kind that get burned as witches.

In contrast, Saturna has attracted journalists. As early as the 1950s, we ink-stained wretches made the epic journey to this awkwardly situated island, fell in love with its freedom from the humbug of the media and bought lots at prices that proved to be an astounding investment. Properly located, misanthropy really pays off.

Most of the Saturna journalists—including me—have been columnists, the crustiest of a sour breed. The island harbours no public-relations people or other writers whose integrity is for sale. No, sir. The intellectual climate of this Gulf Island is such as to say: If you can't say something nice about someone, you're in.

So what is it about an island that attracts writers as well as seaweed? One recalls that the Isle of Wight was home to a colony of nineteenth-century authors, notables such as Alfred Tennyson, Robert Browning, Lewis Carroll and Henry Longfellow.

Not too shabby for an island not all that much bigger than Salt Spring or Saturna, and a big encouragement for those of us who have unpublished verse in our bottom drawer, waiting for the market to improve.

Obviously there is something creative about living

lonesome on the edge of a craggy cliff, overlooking a sea that favours the generation of great literature. But what?

It may be in the blood. Ireland has produced far more writers of note than any comparable area of land surrounded by water generally unsuitable for swimming. As is Saturna. All we lack is Bernard Shaw's literary agent.

Or it could be that the island environment reduces the volume of incoming distractions that characterize life in the city. A partial list:

1. No mail delivery. In town a percentage of our hopes and fears is tied to the daily droppings of the queen's post. Nine times out of ten, what the postie regurgitates from her pouch fails the hopes and feeds the fears. The anticipated cheque isn't there on the floor below the letter slot, but we do pick up the firm reminder from Revenue Canada that it has us by the pendants, plus a card from Cousin Edith advising of her imminent visit and expectation of being accommodated, fed and toured. Very bad for the concentration, that. On the island, however, all mail stays in the post office. In the general store. In boxes, where it belongs. Islanders can pick up their grief when they choose, or are feeling strong and have room enough in their minds for disgust at store flyers, predatory realtors, blandishments and reports from their member of Parliament that confirm their misgivings about democracy as a system of government.

2. No newspaper delivery. This emancipates us from the daily wail. We remain blissfully unaware of the latest human interest story, written to tug at our

heartstrings. Need your heart restrung? Move to the island.

3. No computerized phone calls from people dedicated to cleaning our rugs. No one, Gallup or Trot, tries to poll us on the island. We remain totally unpolled. It's a glorious feeling knowing you're not part of any statistic you're aware of.

4. Finally, and by no means least, we escape the decibel carnage of gas mowers, blowers and stowers, the Harleys howling in rut, noisy overflights of anything but geese, and the neighbour's kid cranking up his stereo to drive more holes into the ozone layer.

Yes, man *can* live by bread alone, if he can eat it while watching TV. The satellite dish makes all types of information and entertainment an option, not an imposition. If I want print that turns yellow overnight, I can buy the Saturday *Globe and Mail* at the store and catch up on the decline of Western civilization.

Otherwise I have a mute button on the world.

Often, driving the freeway to Tsawwassen and the ferry, I pass the glacial flow of Vancouver commuters edging in the opposite direction, mile after mile of multiple-lane vehicles whose drivers are listening to an eye-in-the-sky radio reporter tell them that the traffic is backed up far north and south of the Tunnel—a confirmation that misery has lots and lots of company.

What a waste of life! In order to exercise their independence from public transit, these people spend hours of every working week locked in a bastille of bumpers. For a holiday, they lock into a different queue—at the US border.

I guess it's a change, gazing at a Washington state licence plate.

Compelled attention to locomotion, such as this, isn't suitable for the writer. He needs room to live inside his head, for longer than when he's alone in the office washroom cubicle.

In fact, there is some evidence that having all one's senses is detrimental to the imagination. Consider the blind Homer and Milton, the deaf Beethoven. Well, okay, maybe they went *too* far for us lesser talents. The sensory deprivation we gladly accept is to be out of touch. On the island.

4

The Island Psyche

"**N**o man is an island," wrote John Donne. But some men have a lot of island in them, notably Englishmen. Englishwomen don't seem to have as much island content as the male of the breed. They can be quite happy surrounded by children instead of water. It's the other gender's rogue Brit whose insularity is celebrated by the Bard in *Richard II*:

> . . . this sceptred isle,
> This earth of majesty, this seat of Mars,
> This other Eden, demi-paradise,
> This fortress built by Nature for herself . . .

In contrast, the Frenchman is totally content to be continental. He fails to understand why the English describe the Channel as a body of water separating France from the mainland.

Now perhaps Saturna shouldn't be described as an isle,

sceptred or otherwise. Capri is an isle. Isles are romantic. People go to an isle for their honeymoons. They go to Saturna to recover from their divorces.

The island is characterized by its indigenous vehicles: mostly mean old trucks and vans that keep going out of sheer cussedness. I, however, drive a small red coupe. I do my best to make it unobtrusive on the island. Before I leave town I throw mud on it. Even so, it tends to stick out like a sore thumb, pointed down.

At the Swartz Bay Saturna-bound ferry lineup, I once sat behind a large and ancient van held together by rust and strong language. The bumper sticker read: Beer Is Better Than Women. Beer Never Has a Headache.

I don't even drink beer. Therefore I became acutely conscious of having a bottle of Old Sack sherry sitting on my back seat, carefully camouflaged to look like a small child in swaddling clothes. Because, what if those rugged guys clustered around the van, laughing and sucking their coffin nails, noticed that my licence plate was *clearly legible*? How would my coupe look concertinaed?

Saturna was described in a perceptive magazine article as being "independent, reclusive, anarchic." The island's dyspeptic disposition has well suited the abnormal number of journalists who have bought property on the island for the specific purpose of being prickly.

If cantankerousness were infectious, the whole island would be quarantined.

These newspaper columnists have nothing to do with one another, on the island or off. Their cottages are remote from each other. They constitute a colony of iconoclasts, ready to die rather than admit they have anything in common except contempt for government.

Theoretically this island, like others in the strait, is governed by the provincial legislature in Victoria. But Saturnans never elect a representative who might become a government member. Their member is always in opposition—to everything. If the government introduced a bill to make happiness compulsory, the member for Saanich and the Islands would vote against it—on principle.

Thus the whole of Canada was startled out of its phlegm a while ago when Senator Pat Carney—a former journalist—announced that British Columbia might well consider separation from the benighted East unless Ottawa pulled up its socks well above the present altitude. Senator Carney has long owned a cottage on Saturna. Her readiness to disassociate with the Establishment is perfectly natural. In fact, we other Saturnans are merely bemused that the senator didn't burn the maple-leaf flag on Parliament Hill.

This tone of antipathy was set early on the island by its typical pioneer: the renegade Englishman. Some Canadian pioneers came to the West in a covered wagon, others in a private launch, as did Warburton Pike and Charles Payne. These two sons of well-to-do English families scouted the Gulf Islands in a luxurious forty-eight-foot steam launch dubbed *Saturna* and described by Victoria's *Colonist* as "a shapely little thing," and "fitted with every view to internal comfort."

Warburton Pike set the tone for the Saturna raj. Born in Dorsetshire in 1861, he attended Rugby School and graduated from Oxford. In his definitive history *Homesteads and Snug Harbours*, Peter Murray describes Pike as "a larger-than-life figure, constantly on the move. Although he spent only a brief sojourn on Saturna, he made a lasting impact . . ."

Indeed. The peripatetic squire has an eminence named after him. Mount Warburton Pike is more than an impressive mouthful. At 1,400 feet it is also one of the highest mountains in the Gulf Islands. Today his mountain is topped with the contemporary version of the statue of the Christ figure: a TV transmitter.

This celestial icon broadcasts salvation—originating in station CHEK Victoria—to all the souls in these waters hungry for sitcom and soap. Blessed with the proximity of Mount Warburton Pike, Saturnans have no need for cable. Or bunny ears. Or, I believe, even for a TV set. The radiation is powerful enough to penetrate eye and ear directly. People climb Mount Warburton Pike not only because it is there but because, standing at the summit, they can simultaneously experience a breathtaking panorama of Gulf Islands and a subliminal pitch for Scope mouthwash.

From this crest, one may gaze downward a thousand feet to the forest-girt meadows that once were the ranch of rambler Pike. A bucolic marvel of hundreds of acres, set between Plumper Sound and an escarpment straight out of a Tarzan movie, this spacious glade was so marvellously secluded that ships of Her Majesty's navy used it for gunnery practice in the mid-1900s.

In keeping with his restless ilk, Warburton Pike didn't linger long in his spread. He rarely used the handsome house he had built, his shibboleth being "the best place to sleep is under a tree." He had a favourite western maple of massive girth under whose boughs he liked to bed down.

This concept of "roughing it" still has enormous appeal to Saturna cottagers. We love to expose ourselves to the total experience of the great outdoors, while knowing, in case it rains, there is a comfortable house twenty feet away. That's living.

When awake, Warburton wasn't averse to company. Not that of ladies, however. Women have a tendency to create permanent residence, whether or not this was what a man originally had in mind. They have no flair for being transient. Only eventually did women come to Saturna and other Gulf Islands to do the hard work eluded by the scions of stately English homes. For Pike and his bachelor chums, however, the chosen activity in the fields was a game of cricket. Cannon shot and cricket balls were the projectiles of Britain's empire.

And it was easier to pull up stumps of the wicket sort before the game got serious. The sporty Englishmen came and went, settling briefly on the choice parts of the island, knowing they were unsuited for the commune.

They would have nodded agreement with Jean-Paul Sartre: *"L'enfer, c'est les autres."* If Hell *is* other people, Saturna must be Heaven. Yet it's doubtful the Father of Existentialism would have traded Paris for this paradise, as defined by the absence of anyone else. Most of us, even philosophers, seem to need some degree of companionship, if only to feed *le diable au corps*.

For the eremites who succeeded Pike as the lairds of Saturna Beach, the answer was sheep. One of these settlers, whose travels had taken him to Patagonia, introduced South American cuisine in the form of a lamb fry, held annually for schoolchildren of neighbouring islands. This picnic grew into an international event, each Canada Day, that still draws hundreds of watercraft, American and Canadian, in one huge outburst of conviviality that helps the residents to remain insular for the rest of the year.

The Campbells—Jim and Lorraine—are the sheep farmers who domesticated Warburton's idyll, and proved that married cohabitation is feasible, if not traditional, for people who remember what happened to Paul Gauguin.

Shepherd Campbell has been an inspiration to us all—especially if we are part Border collie.

5

The Pig War

The international border between Canada and the United States, after behaving itself quite reasonably from the Great Lakes to the West Coast, as the forty-ninth parallel, has a fit when it hits the Strait of Georgia. It zigs, then zags, and finally does a flip up Juan de Fuca Strait—a borderline case of the barmy.

This cartographer's nightmare was caused by the need to accommodate the southward sag of Vancouver Island, along with the smaller Gulf Islands, as part and untidy parcel of Canada. In consequence, the ferry from Vancouver (aka Tsawwassen) to the islands cuts through a corner of the line and momentarily plies American waters. Some passengers claim this is the most turbulent phase of the voyage. The ship shudders, they say, and the cafeteria coffee tastes more violent.

I can't say I've noticed this Yankee yawing myself. Waves are waves, to my jaundiced eye, and I've never brooded about the possibility of being drowned in a foreign sea on a doomed *Queen of Nanaimo.*

But we are much more aware of American presence, living in a southern Saturna cottage that looks out upon Haro Strait, its three-mile-wide Boundary Pass and the rather wet border that splits it into the Land of the Free and the Home of the Taxed Silly. The islands opposite ours—the San Juans—are too distant for us to see the Stars and Stripes waving over American cottages. However, we are keenly conscious of the state of Washington in proximity to our state of anxiety.

Somewhere in those San Juans lies a US submarine base. Nuclear subs. Tridents. Pulsing with enough destructive force to ruin our day at the cottage. Sometimes we think we see a conning tower cleaving the strait. We put the glasses on it. (Possibly a big mistake. Those sub captains can be touchy.) But so far, no. It's just a riptide. But we know they are out there, running deep, running silent and running into our front yard, if the skipper has had a bad night.

Our feeling about this closeness to Nuke County is ambivalent. In some ways it's reassuring to live in proximity to so much power, even though none of it can be harnessed to run a washer and dryer. The downside is that, in the event of attack by aliens bent on subduing Earth, the American sub base will be a prime target. If their aim is even a weensy bit off, we on Saturna are roadkill.

This scenario is made even more plausible by the other American clout set in the San Juans: Whidbey Island naval air base. The difference between overflights of their military planes and our military plane is we can hear ours in time to see it. With the American fighter, we are looking at where it was, maybe as recently as last week. I'm sure our cottage is under stratospheric surveillance by planes that can detect me sticking my tongue out at a Washington troller.

However, I give the Americans full credit for unobtrusiveness. Their subs cruise too deep to be seen, and their planes fly too high to be visible. It isn't as though we cottagers at East Point have a constant reminder that we are living on the cusp of Armageddon. In fact, lounging on my deck with a preprandial sherry, I may even toast the Yanks across the chuck.

With reason. One of those San Juan islands whose cottage lights wink at me in the night was the scene of the incident that came within a hog's whisker of putting our two countries at war: the Pig War, that is.

The official name for this porcine kerfuffle is the San Juan Boundary Dispute. It's called a dispute because the only casualty—aside from Canadian geography—was a pig. Name never given. The Unknown Porker.

The story, which I relish telling to guests at the cottage in the knowledge that it will shorten their stay by as much as days, goes as follows. The treaty that settled the Oregon Question—which was the $64 question of 1846—was a bit sloppy. It designated the border between the United States and Canada as a line drawn through the middle of Juan de Fuca Strait. No one noticed—probably because no one looked—that Juan de Fuca Strait bifurcated, after it got east of Victoria, into Haro and Rosario Straits. Between them—straitjacketed, you might say, if you wanted to live dangerously—lay the San Juan Islands, more or less up for grabs.

Never loath to grab what was up, the Hudson's Pay Company, in the form of a sheep farm, occupied San Juan Island. As a branch of the fur trade, this was a stretch. But no excuse was too small to raise the Union Jack over some really prime real estate.

Some Americans, though, lingered about on the island, and in 1859, one such named Lyman Cutler caught an HBC pig stealing his potatoes. He shot the pig, with fatal results. This incensed the HBC, whose representative demanded that Mr. Cutler accompany him to Victoria for prosecution as a swine killer.

Mr. Cutler declined to go. In his eyes, the queen's grunter had invaded his American spuds, and therefore deserved to pay the supreme penalty. He appealed for help from the US Army, which was delighted to arrive in force, armed with cannon and shot, piss and vinegar, and the rest of the spirit of General Custer.

Because the Americans got there fustest with the mustest, the Crown's response was to surround San Juan Island with British warships. Impasse.

Just as well for our side. Reason: the US troops were commanded by George Edward Pickett. Yes, the warrior who rose to the rank of Confederate general and, in the US Civil War, led Pickett's Charge, the highlight of the Gettysburg Campaign in that it resulted in the virtual annihilation of his division of troops.

Had Pickett been killed earlier in a foolhardy charge against the British men-of-war in Haro Strait, it would have changed the whole history of the American Civil War. Abraham Lincoln might not have been moved enough to write the Gettysburg Address. It boggles the mind to realize how the history of nations could have been changed by one pilfering pig.

However, instead of a historic battle, for thirteen years our version of the Bay of Pigs—the Pigs of the Bay—stood at stalemate. Then both parties agreed to arbitration by German Emperor Wilhelm I. With a callous disregard for the rights of our colonial sausage meat, His Imperial

Highness stuck a pin in the map to designate Haro Strait as the international border. This plumped all of the San Juans into the lap of Uncle Sam, a loss still being felt by shoppers on Bay Day.

The kaiser may have got the best of this deal, since a German prince subsequently bought up huge parcels of Saturna and other Gulf Islands, property held in absentia to this day. His heir is without doubt our island's most noble nonresident. Thinking of how much taxes he must be paying to support our roads makes us peasant cottagers grateful enough to drink to the return of the German monarchy.

Still, when I gaze across Boundary Pass at Orcas and San Juan and all the other lovely, smaller islands lost from British Columbia, I have to regret that the Hudson's Bay Company didn't keep that pig in a proper sty. For the want of a leash, the islands were lost. Pity.

6

Legends of the Lost

T umbo. The name rumbles like a Disney character, yet to look at Tumbo today—this 260-acre isle just around the corner from our Saturna cottage—you would never suspect its violent past. No one lives there at the moment. The whole island has been owned by various moneybags who apparently got spooked by the ghosts, decided to spend the night on their yacht and finally sped back home to California, never to return.

Until I learned its history, this boomerang-shaped islet looked idyllic to me, too. Perhaps because *Robinson Crusoe* is my favourite work of fiction, whenever I look upon Tumbo, while driving Tumbo Channel Road, I fancy myself treading the white strand of its cove's beach (said to be the fairest in these parts), waiting for a female Friday to leave her dainty footprint on my mind.

But Tumbo's beckoning smile hides some broken fangs. Its placid aspect conceals the evidence that proves: the smaller the island, the bigger the demons that haunt it. A really large island, such as Australia, may be able to escape with only a mild case of terrors, say, Australian football or those awful flies, but a tiny island creates the mind-set of the castle owner stuck without a drawbridge. His only companion is paranoia.

Such apprehension may have coloured the account of Tumbo's earliest recorded white inhabitant, Ike Tatton, who told of his witnessing a fierce battle between Native tribes from the vantage point of the tree he had prudently climbed. His story certainly gains credibility from the number of human skulls and arrowheads that have gratified beachcombers since Ike did the colour commentary for the aboriginal contest.

Besides human bones, Tumbo was once believed to yield coal. The romance of coal mining was rampant in these parts during the late 1890s. While the Klondike was getting more attention from the media, probably because gold has more mystique than anthracite, men were also seduced by the allure of coal as a fortune maker. Coal fever gripped Vancouver for a time, hence Coal Harbour, whose name remains as a token of unrequited love.

Similarly traces of coal turned the head of Charles Gabriel, manager of a Japanese trading-goods store in Victoria. Convinced that Tumbo Island was a lode of black gold, Gabriel used a buying trip to Japan to enlist the services of a feisty son of Yokohama named Kisuki Mikuni. Mr. Mikuni's qualifications to engage in coal mining were somewhat obscured by his previous occupation as a clerk in a bazaar.

Returning to Tumbo with a recruited workforce of twenty-one men, the intrepid duo started digging their coal mine. A temporary pall was cast over the shaft when the contractor and an engineer were killed by a boiler explosion. Undeterred by ill omen, Gabriel rallied the stygian host and had hit 245 feet down when seawater flooded into the dig. Unable to stanch the Strait of Georgia, Gabriel abandoned his mine, his heroic effort doomed to be totally ignored by Pierre Berton.

With the dreams of fossil-fuelled wealth dead in the water, Tumbo's next resident hallucinator was a German hermit named Barnard Wenzel, whose lebensraum was the west side of the island. On a stormy evening in 1905, another German, John Shultz, sought to shelter his boat in the lee of the island and came ashore to wait out the tempest. He was challenged by Herr Wenzel, who was, apparently, excessively proprietary about the foreshore. The exact words of the conversation aren't available in transcript, but Shultz must have demurred about leaving before the storm had abated. Hence Wenzel's trudging up to his cabin to fetch his gun.

Sensing he had set a new standard in being unwelcome, Shultz got his own gun from his boat and was ready when his hostile host came out firing what may have been a warning shot. Since there were no witnesses to the shoot-out except a few startled gulls, we have only Shultz's word for it that he shot back in self-defence, intending only a loud deterrent.

Shultz then departed, returning to Mayne Island where he roused Justice of the Peace Tom Collinson to report that he had been engaged in a duel by a Prussian fruitcake, who may have been grazed by a ricochet.

Knowing his duty and how to delegate it, Justice Collinson at once dispatched Constable Angus Ego—whose name alone earns him a place among Canadian heroes—in a rowboat. Ego set forth on that still-stormy October morn, rowing stoutly the several miles to Tumbo.

Three hours later he reached the beach of the jinxed isle, where he found, sprawled on the doorstep of Wenzel's cabin, the body of the prickly recluse, dead of a gunshot wound.

Rarely has a murder been so devoid of mystery as to the killer.

Not unsurprisingly no charge was laid against Shultz. The Code of the West prevailed, it seemed. Wenzel had simply been at the wrong place (his), at the wrong time (October). Case closed.

Saturna Island, too, has had its killing field. Murder Point, it's called. A small projection, west side, upon Plumper Sound, its story is bleak, with no redeeming features.

In 1863, having decided to move to Mayne Island, Frederick Marks loaded seven other family members into a small boat and set forth under glowering skies that soon became violent. The boaters' peril was observed by a Mayne Islander, Chris Myers, who rowed his boat to the rescue. With darkness, the two boats became separated. That bearing Marks and his daughter Caroline put into a small cove on Saturna. There, while they sat by their campfire, they were attacked by a band of Lamalchi Natives. They shot the father and chased Caroline into shoreline rocks, where her body was found wedged. Her father's body was never recovered, but his boat was found plundered and smashed to kindling.

Summoned naval vessels tracked the alleged ringleader of the assailants, Umluhanik, to Galiano Island, where he was cowering in a cave. A hair clasp found in his possession was identified as having belonged to Caroline. Subsequently four Lamalchi were convicted of murder and hanged in Victoria in July 1863.

I haven't visited Murder Point. Not being one to seek out sources of depression and/or anxiety, I need no historical reminder that Saturna is part of the aboriginal land claim of at least one tribe, whose present village is on Vancouver Island. Occasionally band members come over to Saturna to shoot deer on their multiacre, pristine reservation and squeeze off a few rounds over the white folks' cottages to serve as a temporary restraining order.

Some cottagers are delighted to find an old stone arrowhead on their property. Not me. The less evidence that my land title is void, the better, to my mind. One of my nightmares is that of digging to level our driveway and hitting a 10,000-year-old Native midden. That proof of ownership would antedate my deed by several weeks.

This is another good reason for my not doing any more spadework than necessary on what I fondly believe to be my property. Nothing has been really settled yet between the Native people and us squatters. True, I may invite an unwanted guest to take a long walk in the Native reservation. But I walk in the opposite direction, wearing my Musqueam band T-shirt, the one with the bright red design of salmon leaping to the Great Spirit.

7

The Secret Vice of Ferry-Watching

It is Polynesia North, but first you have to get to it, which isn't easy. The southern Gulf Islands are a jigsaw puzzle kicked over by a falling angel. Because they are off the reasonably straight line that would be the shortest distance between the two points—Vancouver and Victoria—reaching them can require the taking of several ferries of diminishing size and schizoid schedule.

A couple of the Gulf Islands have been threatened with the building of a bridge to help connect the Mainland with the Big Island. None of the plans has got past the planning stage, because the planners have had crosses burned on their lawns by delegates from whichever island that doesn't welcome becoming a viaduct for motor traffic. It is part of the mystique of every island that the island is the sublime destination, not part of a highway system.

You come, you stay until fulfilled, you leave. No one-night stand in a motel. You *marry* the island, sir, if you know what's good for you.

This commitment is particularly firm for Saturnans. The permanent residents almost relish the plight of us Mainlanders who try to have an affair with the island that lasts less than a lifetime. The need to transfer from a large ferry to a smaller ferry, to sit for hours in various transfer compounds, baking in sun or peering through rain for the vessel delayed by any one of the many afflictions to which the BC Ferry Corporation is prone—these circumstances do much to keep Saturna free of the uncommitted.

There have been case-hardened men who have chosen the French Foreign Legion over signing on for Saturna.

So we summer cottagers are obliged to see the Ferry Experience as a major part of the pleasure—a bizarre type of masochism—or a character builder, in the same class as World War II.

It begins with my having to make a reservation for my car. To do this with any hope at all of retaining a shred of sanity, I must have the current ferry schedule. In my judgement, a large part of the Ferry Corporation's thousands of employees is devoted entirely to changing the ferry schedule. The changes are made after consultation with the Oracle of Victoria, which predicts the seasonal ebb and flow of traffic, with consideration of the influence of the Japanese Current and hunches drawn from a hat.

The obvious place for a person to obtain a copy of the ferry schedule is aboard a ferry. Having to board a ferry in order to obtain the ferry schedule needed to make a reservation to access the ferry: this is how the Ferry Corporation discourages triflers and people who are already hysterical.

In addition—and this may be only a personal observation flawed by paranoia—the schedule pamphlets are placed in parts of the ship not normally seen by the passenger searching for one: in the engine room, under lifeboats, et cetera.

For further backup against its leaking information, as soon as the Ferry Corporation senses that too many would-be passengers are getting hold of the current schedule, it issues a new schedule, with previously unknown constellations of asterisks to ensure that no two days of the week have exactly the same timetable. This schedule is then hidden in new places on the vessels.

The only constant in the car-ferry scheduling is the requirement that your vehicle arrive at the check-in booth at least forty minutes before departure time, which is the stuff of whimsy. Tardiness may be punished by relegation to "standby status," a vehicular kind of Purgatory from which few attain salvation. Whereas the ferry rarely apologizes for leaving late unless summer has turned to fall, the loading crew have little patience with drivers who plead being delayed by gridlock, or a medical emergency such as donating a kidney. In this they have the full support of those of us who have arrived well ahead of the deadline and sit in our cars until turned to stone.

Because of these vagaries of the long wait, it is easy for me, the driver, to doze off, with my hand poised over the ignition key. Not until I jerk awake to see that the cars ahead of me in the line have been waved onto the ferry, hear a public-address voice blaring "Will the small red Honda please proceed?" and note an attendant gesture me forward with an expression of total exasperation, do I panic. I reverse instead of go forward, release wind rather than the brake, try to lower the radio antenna by opening the hood and, at last, lurch forward through a gauntlet of faces clearly not glad to be helping the mentally handicapped.

Barrelling, I catch up with the cars entering the maw of the ferry, just as we hit the speed bumps. These steel ridges rise and fall with the tide, phases of the moon that can neuter a car's suspension system. Watching vehicles try to take the bump too fast—sparks spraying as metal grinds on metal—is one of the more dependable sources of entertainment for the car-deck ferry crew. I've drawn applause more than once.

Now, however, I've learned to traverse the deadly rise as if anticipating the sudden uplift of a tsunami. Disappointment is obvious on the countenances of the crew, but I'm accustomed to being no fun at a party.

Then it's into darkness. I know how Jonah felt, being swallowed into the belly of the whale. Such is your entry into the ferry's car deck. You follow the jittery brake lights of the car ahead, round and round, chancy as the ball in the roulette wheel.

I suspect the Ferry Corporation has me secretly listed as dangerous cargo. Why else would the crew always park me beside a colossal tanker filled with enough propane gas to blow the ship, and possibly me with it, to smithereens?

That highly flammable presence inches from my door persuades me not to remain in my car in company with the dogs and cats and livestock not allowed up on the passenger decks. But the decision to abandon the den isn't made lightly. Reason: it is incredibly easy to be unable to find the car again when it comes time to disembark and partake of an even more frantic panic than that inspired by boarding.

They—the ferry people—hide certain cars, you know. While certain drivers are upstairs, trustingly looking for a schedule pamphlet, they somehow move a car that was parked on Deck 3B up to Deck 2B. That's why I find myself trying to run crazed up a down escalator crowded with other passengers—an aerobic exercise with few redeeming features.

So I write the number of my car deck on the palm of my hand to improve my chances of ever seeing my car again. This means not washing my hands during the voyage. Going to the washroom must be carefully thought out, therefore, if not avoided altogether. It may seem overcautious, wearing Pampers in order to find an automobile, but the sea can be a stern mistress.

This fact is briefly forgotten in the excitement of seeing that the ferry is at last moving out of the jetty. She hoots, sharing my surprise at actual movement. Gazing out the lounge window, on the side that will sun-dry me when the ship, giggling, turns around, I'm moved to capture the moment in verse:

> Time cannot pale,
> nor custom dull,
> the oft-told tale
> of buoy meets gull.

Thus are some of us stirred by the drama of the ship's leave-taking. More, however, head for the cafeteria. It isn't good form for passengers to bring their own grub onboard to save money. That shows no spirit of adventure. It's like packing a chastity belt for a cruise on the Love Boat.

The ferry cafeteria provides a unique experience akin to losing your virginity. You enter this labyrinth whose minotaur is the cashier and file past a spare buffet of sandwiches, muffins and other delicacies, all wrapped for freshness and, indeed, forever. Trying to extract one of these goodies from its plastic carapace helps to pass the time for most of the crossing of the strait.

It also gives you something to do with your hands while you observe other passengers—a fascinating cross section of escapees from urbanization. Most of us read, or pretend to. This way we avoid making eye contact with someone who turns out to be someone we know. Or should know. Like a former lover. Or our proctologist. Someone we ought to care about enough to be able to recognize the moustache.

Passengers who have forgotten to bring the survival kit of books or crossword puzzles may be forced to stand on an outside deck, pretending to be fascinated by a passing dead-head.

I have resorted to this escape manoeuvre myself, inhaling both funnel smoke and that from nicotine addicts obliged to puff outside and fume in more ways than one. To be free of all annoyance, you may be required to stand at the bow of the ship, leaning into the wind until your eyebrows blow off.

For me, having my vision impaired by salt spray makes it harder to interpret the symbols on the doors of the ferry's rest rooms. These have been designed to minimize any appearance of gender discrimination. The female symbol (skirted) and the male symbol (panted) are barely distinguishable, especially if the ship is rolling. Yet I dare not loiter at the door, peering at a hieroglyphic. Guys have been arrested for harassing the Ladies, which is why I pause only briefly and may run several laps around the deck for confirmative glimpses before actually entering the washroom.

Once in, I hate to leave it. But how many times can a guy comb his hair?

Then, hey, we're there! Arriving at the island! Moment of

climax! We sit in our cars, waiting for the ecstasy to begin. For, truly, 'tis better to have felt your ferry dock than never to have loved at all . . . the penetration of bow 'twixt pilings . . . the erection of the landing platform . . . the repeated impact that gives release to our hand brake . . . then, ejaculation! One last bump and grind up the ramp and we are off to the womb of our island home.

Ferry delayed? Think of it as coitus interruptus. Euphoria is only a ship's whistle away.

8

The Specs of Shangri-la

I t often starts in a sleeping bag, alone or in company. We are out camping and we come upon this charming bit of hinterland, then jump up to cry, "This is it! This is where I want to build my dream cottage and escape from the city's pollution, crime and all the other modern inconveniences."

We take photos. We remove the For Sale sign and hide it under leaves. And we take care, when contacting the property owner, to sound slightly indifferent, though we are prepared to mortgage our firstborn.

This is virtual realty. Its basic principle: never buy cottage property primarily as an investment. To harbour even a hint of such tawdry purpose in our minds dooms the property to become worthless overnight. Right now it may be hard to imagine that the lot next to ours will be acquired by the US Atomic Energy Commission to entomb nuclear waste. But it will happen.

No, our hearts must be as pure as the country air when we sign the agreement to purchase. Mind you, it doesn't hurt to do a bit of independent research into how the area's properties have appreciated in value over recent years. This may mean asking your realtor to take a polygraph test. The test is now available at some of our larger drugstores and is said to be accurate fifty percent of the time.

Some people think that, because they are buying land out in the country, they should hire a country lawyer to handle the legal aspects of their ripping off the vendor. Then they are disappointed when their country lawyer refuses to have his fee paid in eggs or sacks of potatoes. The unfortunate fact is that both realtor and legal fees must be factored in, using dollars rather than rural produce, when reckoning the total cost of acquiring that little outpost of Elysium.

However, once we have a firm grasp on the fact that the cottage is going to cost more than we can afford, we can go ahead and enjoy being ravished. As in other romances, the foreplay is often more pleasurable than the consummation. The major turn-on is: everyone wants waterfront, on sea, on lake, on creek, or at the very least on an upscale puddle.

True, some folk profess to prefer having their cottage fronting on a dry gulch, which *was* a river until the hydro company built the dam. But that's mere rationalizing. These people are just too chicken to build a cottage that is beyond their means. Hardly the pioneer spirit.

But why do we have this great craving for the sight, and sound, of water? Is it something in the blood that cries out for the primordial aquatic milieu whence we emerged? Or are we ecstasied by the ever-changing moods of ocean and pond? Or is it simple joy in gazing at something we don't have to mow?

Whatever. But it is the desideratum of a view of the drink that can make the property seeker a sucker for swampy ads. "Access to the beach," for instance, is broadly interpreted by realtors. Any place within ten miles of a barnacle-rife beach qualifies as "waterfront property." As in buying a car, a person should check the mileage on the access before diving off the front deck.

On the Gulf Islands, the waterfront is likely to be at the bottom of a 100-foot cliff. You don't just sprint from your atoll *bure* across a coral strand to wade into the blue lagoon. Our beach is more of a hop, skip and a parachute jump to access. Our waterfront cottage on Saturna Island is typical, in that I have never seen the waterline, and my ever reaching it depends on a rappelling skill I may be too old to master.

However, the big plus in owning waterfront property atop a precipice is that we are spared the nuisance of strangers traipsing across "our" beach. The only noisy beach parties are held by sea lions whose rock music is that of breakers on limestone. For humans the waters of Boundary Pass are too cold, and turbulent with tide, for swimming by any but orca and duck, ideal conditions for us who are natatorially challenged.

We were, in fact, so dazzled by the briny prospect that we neglected to notice the absence of water known as potable—"and not a drop to drink." Gulf Islanders are kin to the Ancient Mariner, a relationship to be explored in a later chapter.

For now let us assume that you have found the summer cottage site of your dreams and have convinced your family that your life savings would not be better spent if fed into a high-speed shredder. What to do next?

First define your terms. What *is* a cottage? The word derives from the Olde English *cote*, an animal shelter. The cottage is a designer sheepcote. Anything larger is a house. Yet a summer house is smaller than a summer cottage. Unless you are Olde English, this confusion will be added to the cost of construction.

It is possible that your chosen site already has a cottage on it. More likely just the basement. The realtor may explain that this concrete bulk is the ruin of an ancient aboriginal civilization, which should enhance the value of the property. The truth is that the previous cottage owner got depressed and in a drunken stupor kicked over an oil lamp, cremating himself and his cote.

Whether it's a relic basement or a whole hut that's ghosting the site, you should hesitate to incorporate the structure into your plans. The result is apt to look like something out of a Stephen King novel. This may serve as a repellent to thieves and squatters, but if your cottage is haunted by a moaner killed by his mortgage—false economy.

Everything considered, it is better to build your cottage from scratch. This will require more scratch than you thought. No matter how much you allow for unanticipated costs, these always exceed the estimate by roughly $100,000. But not to fret. You are choosing a very satisfying way of going bankrupt.

Should you build the cottage yourself? This, too, is iffy. Some people—mostly men—are confident that, because they once built a doghouse that their dog accepted after being severely beaten, they can build a summer cottage with their own hands. If so tempted:

- Examine your hands carefully. Are the fingers all thumbs? Will they look better when thinned out a bit?

- Do you have the requisite tools to build a cottage? That is, something besides your hammer and Book of Common Prayer?

- What do you understand about operating power tools without a source of electricity? Do you own a generator other than the one in your briefs?

- Does your accident insurance cover sawing yourself in half?

To minimize the complications of construction, some people buy a prefab cottage. This is delivered as a load of logs cut to fit together and make a cabin like the one that gave Charlie Chaplin such a bad time in *The Gold Rush*. Assuming that you can hire an Indian elephant to help you assemble the log cabin, you can expect to have one log left over. The one marked Foundation.

On release from hospital, the wiser person will find someone else to build his cottage. It's chicken, yes, but I'll vouch for getting a more livable hen coop.

9

How to Build It Yourself with Help

"Houses are built to live in, and not to look on," Francis Bacon wrote in his essay "Of Building." That's doubly true of the summer cottage. Bringing in a pricey architect to design your cottage is like ironing your underwear. No one else is likely to be looking on it unless you're silly enough to have company.

"If a man: have several dwellings," adds Sir Francis, "that he sort them so, that what he wanteth in the one he may find in the other." Ergo, your city dwelling has the garage; your summer cottage has the peace of mind. It is madness to duplicate the Jacuzzi, for instance, where sensuous pleasure can be had by a good roll in the dust.

With this creative freedom, the potential cottager draws up his own plan for the sanctuary. Anyone can do this. All you need is a sharpened pencil, a ruler, a sheet of drafting paper heavy enough to take repeated erasures, and a photo of Camp David.

Now remember: Rome wasn't built in a day. I know why. Romulus and Remus had to get a building permit. They spent years trying to get their plans of Rome approved by the regional planning department. Draining the marshes was easy, once they got the okay from the plumbing inspector.

So, before you start building *your* place, try to establish your property lines. You really don't want to draw the ground plan for a cottage forty feet wide if you have a thirty-foot lot. It can be off-putting later when your neighbour puts a fence through your bathroom.

But property lines are notoriously elusive. They are identified by stakes driven into the ground when God was a pup, and since overgrown by poison ivy, stinging nettles or a nightshade called vampire's revenge. Property owners should *never* go looking for the stakes without first informing search-and-rescue authorities of their intent to get lost.

Having confirmed that the property is smaller than originally thought when it was bought—wide at the wrong end and short on the view side—the planner can make a rough sketch of the cottage that must be built around the unsuspected twenty-ton boulder.

It was at this point that I conceded defeat and turned the design project over to a reputable contractor. Yes, I did feel the shame of the draft dodger. But when your crayons keep breaking under the pressure, and your language matches the blueprint, prudence dictates a dignified surrender to avoid the rout of all self-respect. Get a contractor.

Island building contractors are a very special breed. Most of them are refugees from city conformism. They are, at heart, artists, like the rest of the poets, painters and pottery makers that populate the Gulf Islands so thickly that wearing a necktie can incur immediate deportation to the Mainland.

If pressed, island building contractors will build "to code," but their hearts won't be in it. What gives them creative satisfaction—and hopefully will also please clients—is adding the byzantine touches that distinguish the cottage from the "monster" house of the city, the Saturday Night Special, and indeed any traditional style that doesn't combine the aesthetic values of the Taj Mahal and a hypertrophic tree house.

Anyway, it was my good fortune to be accepted by the Charles R. (Chuck) Alp Construction Company, a contractor with a deep and abiding contempt for the conventional. To describe Chuck's high standards as alpine would be to cheapen a phenomenon. This hands-on builder and his crew have consistently built houses so uncompromising in materials and workmanship that his profit margin is minuscule. Clients accustomed to the brigandage of urban developers are baffled by the Alp work ethic. Some of them are even forced to revise their whole moral tenet that only man is vile.

Here let me rhapsodize for a moment about the quality of the island tradesman. He, and sometimes she, has enormous self-esteem. This comes with being the definite article. That is, being *the* carpenter in the village, rather than *a* carpenter in the city. In town, today, the young tradesman is likely to be a body in transition, his drain-repair job a sometime thing until he can make it as a rock star/screenwriter/ballet dancer. But it was *the* village blacksmith who took professional pride in making horseshoes that stayed on the horse. Even the village idiot enjoyed community recognition, more than a metropolitan moron, ignored until elected to public office.

"He had rather be first in a village," Bacon reported Julius Caesar as saying, "than second in Rome." (He chose Rome, but it may have shortened his life.) Today our Caesars eye the global village, but there's no global plumber to grace it.

For us, Chuck Alp built a cottage of classic symmetry, its main feature being a wondrously long, shipless deck. It is possible to go for a long, spirited walk without leaving this deck, which cries out for a commodore's hat on the occupant. Games of shuffleboard and deck tennis are quite feasible, should we become demented by the nautical ambience.

To stand at the deck rail, watching the breeze ripple the wild barley grass, is to enjoy the sensation of being a cruise passenger, without having to remember to take a Gravol.

With most of our cottage devoted to the deck, the interior is smallish but easy to operate. The floor plan for the left side of the cottage is exactly the same as the floor plan for the right side of the cottage. No favouritism here. And the design yielded the unique feature of twin flights of stairs, each mounting to a single bedroom. To get from one upstairs bedroom to the other, a person must descend one staircase and climb the other. Good exercise, and a mild contraceptive.

As for interior rooms, my budget obliged Chuck to choose between a large closet or a kitchen. We wisely opted for the kitchen. It is a Pullman kitchen, so named after the railway car that requires the chef to be no more than thirty-two inches in circumference. The advantage of this Pullman kitchen is that everything—sink, stove, fridge, counter, cupboards, needle and pentobarbital—is within arm's reach for an adult orangutan. Similarly the compact bathroom and shower stall make it easy to towel off and clean the window at the same time.

Sinks and cupboards—virtually indestructible—are those rescued from demolition of other cottages. What a story our washbasin could tell! And sometimes tries to. Or at least *some*thing in the plumbing talks in its sleep.

Such is the modest yet perfect cottage that Chuck built— the basics sound, the potential vast. All that remains for us to do is to choose a name for the cottage. This, I feel strongly, is the responsibility of the cottage owner. It is his or her chance to add the final creative touch to this precious asylum from the manic metropolis.

In town your address is simply a number on the house or apartment. That won't do for our cottage, which has an identity beyond the prosaic numerals. The driveway begs for notice of distinction. Nameplates such as Bide-a-Wee and Dun Roamin symptomize an imagination that was stunted at birth. The island expects the cottager to do better. Wit's End and Paradise Leased and their cute like cheapen the investment and are likely copyrighted somewhere in the United States.

The safest sign is the cottager's name: The Smiths. Or, if identification isn't desirable, for reasons known to Revenue Canada, A.N. Other is presentable, if carved on a nice cedar plaque with a sprig of pine cones.

Whichever, the cottage sign is one job that owners really should do themselves. Contempt is easy to come by among the island's tradesmen. It pays to show them that the cottager isn't entirely helpless. Money can't buy their respect. It can buy everything else, of course, but the pioneer spirit still lives on the island, though it doesn't get into town much.

This is why, when I sense that these true islanders are in the vicinity of our cottage, I make a display of simple industry. It may only be my chopping wood, or at least swinging an axe at something hard enough to make a pioneer sound. Or I lug rocks away from our driveway, lugging them back again after dark.

And any visiting islander will likely find me at the outdoor worktable, labouring over the slab of cedar that will eventually be chiselled with The Nicols.

I don't expect this project to be completed in my lifetime. No matter. I'm sure that my children will carry on with the work, much as King Cheops's kids kept puttering away at his pyramid. We all hope to leave something to posterity.

10

The Sanctum

Minimalism, reports the hip press, is the decor of the cognoscenti entering the third millennium.

I'm ahead of my time, again, by God. Our cottage's outhouse represents the minimalest plumbing the neoascetic could wish for.

Here I got dead lucky. Ours was one of the last cottages in these parts to get the permanent-occupancy permit—holy writ to any vendor—with no sewage system but a hole in the ground, sheltered by a clapboard phone booth where only nature calls.

Today you have to install a septic tank. A septic ulcer is grief enough, so who wants to till a septic field, which can lay waste to both environment and your bank account? A septic tank must be emptied regularly by a masked bandit who drives an unmarked truck and refuses to answer any question, including "Who do you like in the World Series?"

No one gets nostalgic about a septic tank. Regardless of

how many years people live with their tanks, there is no emotional bonding. Real love never develops. As with your relationship with the telephone company, your affair with the septic tank is something that fills a functional need yet fails to gain affection.

In contrast, the outhouse speaks its own special poetry to gain our attachment. Only part of its personality is caught by the Merriam-Webster definition of *privy*: "a small building having a bench with holes through which the user may defecate or urinate."

"Small building" captures none of the timeless architecture of the privy. A doll's house is a "small building," well suited to the fantasies of little girls. But the outhouse spurns the gingerbread, as its chaste lines, gently sloping roof and uncluttered entrance combine in the perfect harmony that makes it the Parthenon of closets.

"A bench with holes"?—what a summary account of the privy's austere banquette! *Hockey players* sit on a bench. Judges, we are led to believe, sit on a bench. But to describe the seating arrangement in the outhouse as "a bench," with or without holes, misses the historic drama of this throne of the common man.

Nor is the hole mere frivolous chic. The opposite of the doughnut, the hole is more important than its surround. And like the sun and death, the privy's hole may not be looked upon. That ghastly spectacle will surely remind the evacuator that the noblest work of God still has bugs in the exhaust system.

Yes, it is humbling, the outhouse. It mortifies the flesh, especially in winter. But no other means of evacuation is as environment-friendly. The privy fouls no river or lake with sewage. It kills no fish. What sprang from the soil is returned to it, and only awaits the future's root to find it with joy and exultation.

Another wonder: the outhouse is one of the few kinds of accommodation today that don't require a lock. All it needs is a good singing voice. In my opinion, the pleasant informality of this retreat is spoiled by an outhouse latch that activates Occupied or Vacant. Better to risk the element of surprise, surely, than to remind a guest of that harrowing flight to Cancún.

A confession: when alone at the cottage, I sometimes permit myself the slightly risqué pleasure of using the privy with the door wide open. I don't recommend this for people who have already been arrested for indecent exposure and don't want to extend their rap sheet. But I am clean, I think, and welcome a chance to live dangerously.

What better way to start the morning than seated in contemplation of sunlit forest or limpid lake? Why would I deny myself the unique experience of exchanging gazes with a foraging deer, which seems bemused by how much trouble this biped—which has dropped the lower half of its hide—must go to in order to defecate?

And how could I improve on announcing my presence to the matinal world than with the assertive thud of turd on Mother Earth, drawing echo from the hills, resonant as Julie Andrews's sound of music?

A salutary exercise, gratifying, yet humbling, when compared to the decorous deer scat. A crude ritual, ours, with its attendant deforestation in the cause of marketing the ultimate toilet paper. It is too easy for the person who has been anointed by the bidet of an expensive Paris hotel room to get delusions of functional grandeur. With or without the full frontal nudity, the outhouse represents a happy medium between effete preciosity and the stark brutality of the Arab toilet.

Yet another virtue of this superbly detached house: the privy is the ideal sanctum for a quiet read. Countless men and women who later achieved greatness established their literacy in this homely carrel, this monk's cell that serves the mind as well as the body. Abe Lincoln, log-cabined in frontier Illinois, almost certainly grounded a law career with his reading in the jakes. Often the toilet paper doubled as literature, a versatility lost to modern tissue. Old newspapers and, especially, the Eaton's catalogue broadened the intellectual horizon of people otherwise deprived of the printed word.

Lord Chesterfield, in his *Letters to His Son*, prescribed the proper reading for the privy: short pieces, such as Latin poets, that can be perused in less than eight minutes. Hence the limerick by Anonymous, that celebrated author of the genre:

> There was a young fellow named Chivy
> Who, whenever he went to the privy,
> First solaced his mind,
> Then wiped his behind,
> With some well-chosen pages of Livy.

Frank Muir, creator of the definitive *A Book at Bathtime*, documents the role of the corncob as the predecessor of paper in the privies of America. Whether or not this function was related to the enormous popularity of popcorn in the American Midwest, the anal whisk is less commonly grown on the West Coast. I would furnish our outhouse with a rack of corncobs only if expecting guests who had invited themselves.

I certainly don't tempt fate by putting a surplus copy of one of my own books in our outhouse. Critics lurk everywhere. And I could share the umbrage of the seventeenth-century English poet Robert Herrick, who prefaced his sole volume of verse, *Hesperides*, with a curse:

> Who with thy leaves shall wipe (at need)
> The place, where swelling Piles do breed:
> May every Ill, that bites, or smarts,
> Perplexe him in his hinder-parts.

I also point out to guests that—as preached by the pope of privydom, Chic Sale, in his books *The Specialist* and *I'll Tell You Why*—the right path is designed to require the votary to pass the woodpile. Constipation notwithstanding, the trip can be made worthwhile by his picking up a couple of sticks of firewood.

I admit: the glory of the necessary house is diminished slightly by its becoming more distant on dark, wet nights. This can be especially arduous for the older supplicant, who may be summoned several times in what are called, chillingly, the wee hours. Stumbling, by flashlight, through undergrowth that has waited until dark to grow Amazonian takes some of the curse off indoor plumbing costs.

In winter, particularly, the threat of being frozen to the seat is competitive, as a horror, with the claustrophobia of a commercial jetliner's john.

The traditional, and practical, alternative to this nocturnal expedition is, of course, the commode, aka thundermug. Granted, its chamber music may fall ill on the ear of your companion. (Some sociologists rate the potty tinkle as the ultimate test of a relationship.) The appliance cannot be equipped with a silencer, which puts a lot of pressure on the sphincter to try to reduce the raucous torrent to a trickle. The usual admonition—"Don't try this at home"—isn't effective in this exercise, since most hotels and motels today provide indoor conveniences that deny toilet training for cottagers.

My own choice for muted micturition after midnight is the urinal. No, kids, I don't take one of those men's-room stalls to bed with me. This is a *portable* urinal, the kind the hospital nurse hands you, reluctantly, when you point out that your walking to the bathroom is unrealistic because your broken leg is in traction.

I sleep with my urinal on the floor close to my bed. But not *too* close. A loaded urinal is a disaster waiting to happen. Lacking the stability of the piss pot, it is readily knocked over, causing a flood of biblical proportion. Sleepwalkers should never use a urinal. Certainly not in our cottage.

Here I must add another cavil, based on gender: the urinal is a man thing; the bedpan is a woman thing. This is why men refuse to use a bedpan in the hospital. It destroys their masculinity, whereas the urinal embraces it. But neither should ever be used as a substitute for normal sex.

The remaining problem with both chamber pot and urinal: where to dispose of the contents? For centuries the answer was easy: pitch the waste out the window, preferably when a bill collector was walking on the pavement below. But our summer cottage lacks the adjoining street. To heave-ho the night dew onto the sloping roof that feeds our cisterns would make for tea of a compromised pekoe. It must be transported by daylight to the privy as a solemn offering to the dawn.

Such are the exercises that build character. It is to the outhouse that this nation owes several vertebrae of the moral backbone we associate with Prairie folk. The privy's princedom—Alberta, Saskatchewan, Manitoba—is home to people who accept hardship as part of that short walk to the grave. They are more upright for that sitting, which cannot be said of citizens in cities like Toronto and Vancouver, who have succumbed to sewers, and where bathrooms are often not only indoors but ornate chambers of decadent luxury. There the moral fibre is apt to be rabbit fur, readily shredded by fate.

This is why our cottage will never dismantle that chapel out back. Although I may one day be seduced by my neighbour's indoor composting toilet, which he says is the cat's meow, I shall preserve the privy as a humble reminder that it is, truly, the holy of holeys.

11

Living Without the Mute Button

"Gee, it's so quiet!" So exclaims the visitor when he or she first stands on our cottage deck and notes the absence of the city's hum and haw.

Actually it's not quiet at all. Once the ear comes out of its shell, it can intercept the messages that get lost on cable.

Bird calls, for example.

These start as the matinal chorus that accompanies my trudge to the privy. I realize the birds aren't singing out of joy at seeing that my bladder is still functioning with a degree of control on their property. No, the robins and the finches chirp in declaration of territory. What they are lyricizing is: "Eff off!"

But they say it much more musically than my warning off Jehovah's Witnesses in town.

The percussion section of this avian concert is our woodpecker. The resident flicker drums his riffs on one of the very dead trees that I'm happy to preserve to provide both housing and good termite-hunting for the Gene Krupa of the woods. The flicker also utters a resonant screech, from time to time, to alert all persons with a wooden leg.

Another ground hopper, but with a wistful call, is the towhee, whose name says it all. A shy bird, is the towhee, that scuffles about on the forest floor for unconsidered trifles. This bird is a master, or mistress, of concealing her nest egg, a role model for all of us beset by Revenue Canada.

Anything but plaintive is the majestic *urk* of the bald eagle. Here is a bird of prey that finds no need to have a pleasing voice. It may be that, when mating, bald eagles modify their *urk* to be less peremptory, but I have never overheard their pillow talk.

The eagle's wings spellbind. Surely one of the most transfixing sounds in nature is that sudden *whumpf, whumpf* literally out of the blue. The eagle flies overhead, and I duck, instinctively. Don't tell me that I'm too large to be carried off by an eagle. I've lost weight working at the cottage. To a really peckish bald eagle, I might look a lot like a pink salmon with feet.

To help disabuse our resident eagle—the nest is just down the road a way—I have talked to the bird on occasions when he has perched on the top branch of the big fir directly in front of the cottage, and I'm sitting on the deck. The conversation goes something like this.

"Hi, Milord Eagle! I trust you have feasted well this morning, and that your honouring me with your presence has nothing to do with your keen eye for what may be shortly scavenged."

The bald eagle says nothing. Pretends to ignore me, in fact. Much of the nobility of this symbol of American might lies in his haughty mien. He can be as dumb as dirt, yet people will regard him with awe if he looks too eminent to comment. That is why Supreme Court judges wear black robes and white wigs. They resemble nine bald eagles perched in a row and occupied with withholding judgement.

But I know this bald eagle is hearing me, so I ask him, "Does it bother you, sir, to be called 'bald' when your head is, in fact, fledged and, like mine, white with the wisdom of your years?"

Again, no overt sign that I've struck a nerve with this splendid raptor. I sense he's waiting for me to take his photo. There are so many wildlife films being shot for the insatiable TV audience, it's a rare eagle that hasn't had his natural hauteur caught with his presenting his better profile to the camera.

"Sorry," I say. "I left my camera in town."

Without so much as a nod of civility, the bald eagle swoops away.

I get more attention from the turkey vulture. I can understand why he's hovering over me, the ugly redneck bastard. It's when he winks that bothers me.

More alarming, pound for pound, is the hummingbird. One of these little buzz bombs tried to assault my wife, Mary. She was sunning prone on a pallet on our deck, easing an ache with the red hot-water bottle placed on her nape, when this rufous rapist darted up to the neck of the bottle and tried to extract nectar. Cute, but the bird is too big for its britches. Being able to fly backward may get you invited to parties, but the hummingbird lacks good manners.

Never mind. I can still enjoy the waxy utterance of the martins, putting on their dazzling displays of the right stuff to bag a bug. The cliff swallows can turn on a dime and give you eight cents change—the last word in fast food.

So spectacular are the aerobatics of the martin that it's easy to miss the quiet exchanges of the little waterfowl that bob in the tide's ripple. They are a pair. A male and, I'd guess, a female. A thoroughly domesticated couple, these harlequin ducks, that keep conversation to a minimum, yet never get too far separated as they dive for whatever serves ducks below the salt. Often they are the only life out there on the chuck in a storm that has driven all other surface craft to shelter. In turn, each briefly flutters aloft to check on the other obscured by the whitecaps. Yes, watching a duo of ducks is good marriage counselling and should be required of people contemplating divorce, especially if they have ducklings.

I can't say the same for the herring gull's raucous mewing. The gull has never got over his poetic reputation as the voice of the sea, lamenting the death of drowned sailors. The bird overdoes it. A bit of sad caterwauling goes a long way if the hearer is already having a bad-hair day. And, really, there haven't been all that many sailors drowned in these waters lately. Maybe the gull is keening over the victims of some other natural disaster—the federal government, say, or the introduction of fast ferries that make it tough for a gull to bum a scrap—but this isn't made clear.

What *is* clear, if you're floating about in a boat in Boundary Pass, is that this is no place to have a heated argument with your partner. People don't seem to realize how far voices carry across water. This acoustic phenomenon has provided considerable entertainment for me, lounging on the cottage deck and picking up the conversation of boaters well offshore.

A couple of recreational fishermen in a putt-putt exchange lies that I overhear without batting an ear. Or, from the elegant cruiser idling below my cliff come the groans of amatory activity. When the lady at last emerges from the cabin, adjusting her skirt, and notices me grinning on my deck, she gives me the finger, and we have excellent communication without the long-distance charge.

Replete with the sounds of day, at dark I lay me down in my cottage cot, and it is the cottage that wakes. With creaks and mutterings. With pops and crackles. With overhead rustles, as of bands of marching mice wearing army boots.

Ghosts? But no one has died here. Surely departed spirits are not squatters?

Then the penny drops.

The cottage is simply cooling off after the expansive mood induced by the sun's beaming. The metal roof is contracting. The timbers are cracking their knuckles, the ceiling adjusting its molecules to the cooler air of evening.

But, by heaven, what a medley of crepitation! A concerto for rice cereal and milk! How may I exploit these weird effects to deter guests from overstaying their visits longer than one night? ("Ah, yes, the night noises. We're thinking of having the cottage exorcised if we can persuade a priest to come over from town . . .")

In wintry weather, the cottage roof expresses itself even more dramatically. Overhanging boughs of pine trees suddenly let go their accumulated snow, a benign bomb that puts paid to idle daydreams. At Christmas it's easy to believe that Santa has landed on the roof in a dump truck. I, too, get airborne.

In strong breezes, those same conifers become wood-winds. They sough. Onomatopoeic word that, though I'm not sure whether *soughing* rhymes with *sowing* or *sawfing*. Maybe *surfing*? The same wind sends combers breaking over beach and bough.

When the gusts reach gale force, they find a small crevice in the cottage exterior that produces a shrill whistle, as attention-getting as any blown by cop, referee or cheap dentures.

Such are the sounds of cottage life. Unlike the city, where the ear is so assailed by background noise that it loses its power to discriminate, the cottage is where every whisper gets respect. The ear regains its role as a primary sensor. It positively blooms. Since I can prick up my ears—using muscles I'm proud to share with dogs and deer and other good listeners—I can exercise them here.

It sure beats weightlifting. And it helps me hear the most moving oratorio of all, the one that jerks me out of my chair, or bed, no matter how often I've heard it: the awesome breath of the orcas.

12

Free Willy But Not Near Me

"Thar she blows!"

I have never actually exclaimed this myself, but whoever said it first, said it best. What a wondrous beast is the whale, able to make its presence known just by breathing! *My* breath attracts attention only if there was garlic in my gruel. But the orca's exhalation is a respiratory showstopper. It boggles my wits, as some primal receptor in my cortex recognizes the approach of a family member of the largest creature on Earth. Make way! That behemoth may be ducking for salmon, but I wouldn't choose to swim along, especially in silver trunks.

No matter how many times I've heard that mother of all snorts, I react to it with delight. I hail each pod of killer whales doing their parabolic thing through Boundary Pass in front of our cottage during the seasons when sockeye and coho and pink are making their massive run to the coastal rivers.

The drill is the same for all the cliff's cottagers who hear the stentorian summons: jump into the car, or onto the bike, or run like hell to the lighthouse at East Point. We know the orcas will cut that corner to hang a left up the Strait of Georgia. Their hugging the curve of sandstone cliff brings them as close to shore as the observer would wish without extending his accident insurance.

On the rocky foreshore we gather, eyes peeled for the approaching pod. All the members of that family are now named and numbered and better known than we mere humanoids gawking at them. If *I* were to be harpooned, flensed and sold to Japanese sushi lovers, it wouldn't cause a ripple among conservationists. But those six or eight whales plowing the pass have the right of way so broadly that I stand at least twenty feet back from the waterline, lest one of the older, nearsighted orcas mistakes me for a seal with a death wish. I'm loaded with cholesterol.

The extra dimension to observing the killer whales in person, and in their element, is that—unlike seeing them in a PBS nature film or at Marine World—their sudden, pulse-revving projection from the water is unpredictable. We see the whale submerge *there*, to rear up . . . *where?* This leviathan is the despair of the photographer. Not only does this single-minded mammal not pose to say "Cheese," but it remains submerged for minutes at a time, reappearing half a mile away, just long enough for the camera wielder to get a blurred image of cetacean snot.

The orca cleaves the deep as silent as a knife through butter, then—*bam!*—explodes out of the blue with a sound to shake a homo sap to the very fundaments of fright.

So forget the video camera, the binoculars, the telescope on tripod. Two legs are quite sufficient, two eyes more than enough to enjoy the splendour of the killer whales romping past our lighthouse rock. Yes, they do seem to show off. I see no other explanation for that abrupt, unrehearsed belly flop. The whale is cavorting. It knows somehow that I'm watching with profound respect for its power and beauty. And it says, "Hey, dweeb, here's another big splash you'll never make!"

We know that whales have a sophisticated vocal communication with one another—squeals and other succinct comments beyond the pathetic auditory range of us survivors of rock music. I can't hear it, but I don't doubt the big male orca is remarking to another pod member: "Get a load of that beach litter wearing a white hat! We aquatic mammals didn't return to the sea a moment too soon."

And Big Daddy breaches big-time, secure in his homophobia.

Schmack!

I have another fraction of a second to take in the incomparable contour and colouring of this animal that inspired so much of Haida art.

Some animals seem made to remind humans that, as a simian species, they have paid a dreadful price for their larger brains. The "fearful symmetry" that William Blake exclaims of in the tiger, equally awesome in the orca, bears in upon me that I am descended from a baboon. Despite our claim to be cast in the mould of God and Calvin Klein, how many of us can rightly compare ourselves to the perfect lineaments of the truth in black and white—the killer whale?

Even more than the behemoth grays and blues, whose sheer size mocks our puny weight, the orca models graceful dynamics flagged by that majestic dorsal fin. All I've got on *my* back is a mole.

No wonder the pod has a retinue of whale watchers. Boats of various sizes and shapes loiter in the wake or—suicidally—in the path of the whales. Voyeurs all, are the people in those vessels, their cameras cocked for the home video that will stultify untold hundreds of trapped house guests: "It's a bit fuzzy, but that ring of ripples is where this huge whale practically dived under our boat. This next shot shows Marge pointing to where these two whales were before I dropped the camera . . ."

The orcas seem remarkably tolerant of these vulcanized rubberneckers. Unlike me, who dislikes having people stare when I'm eating, let alone trying to take my picture, the whales proceed with equanimity. They never charge a boat. Although a whale could be excused for mistaking a kayaker for an extra large and clueless cod, they trouble to distinguish.

Indeed, orcas may even enjoy having spectators. Some of these whales are old enough—they can live to fifty or more—to have become hams. Or, being intelligent enough to sense they are now a protected species, they may feel they owe it to us somewhat evolved vermin to perform their boffo ballet.

More likely, though, is that sheer exuberance is what motivates that massive *tour en l'air*. The whale would do it even if I weren't watching. But I applaud, just in case.

13

When Big Is Ugly

W hen orcas aren't plying Boundary Pass and drawing their gallery of gawkers, that broad expanse of the deep can be remarkably boatless. When one considers the numerous marinas choking the inner harbours of the Lower Mainland and the islands of Puget Sound, all the cabin cruisers and sailing craft that strain at their moorings for a go at the briny—wha' hoppen?

Why can I sit for hours at a time on the cottage deck, with the sea smiling invitation, yet I see scarce a single pleasure boat to write its wake on that blank page?

For thousands of boat owners—who have bought their commodore caps and have fitted their bowsprits with bikinied blondes tanned to travel—their boats seem to represent the opportunity to get away from the loony world of landlubbers, to go head-to-head with King Neptune without the need to actually leave the dock. Their boats are something to work on lovingly, great places to hoist a drink, but raising their anchors complicates the dream with some rude aspects of reality.

Sour grapes? Not owning a boat myself, I readily cock a snoot at those martini mariners. And when a brave little putt-putt potters into view . . . I give it a nice hand:

> Alone, alone, all, all alone,
> Alone on a wide, wide sea!
> And never a soul took pity on
> My soul in agony . . .

I'm glad to see that some damn fool—not me—has dared to venture out of the marina to challenge tidal currents that make old Charybdis look like a millpond. At times the whole Pacific Ocean tries to squeeze into Juan de Fuca Strait, and thereafter Boundary Pass, which drains like the Devil's own bathtub, causing the terrified boater to pray for a divine plug.

This is why, when I hear the thrum of a ship's engine out in that corseted sea, it is likely to be propelling a craft weighing more than 20,000 tons. I have become a connoisseur of large freighters. The big boys are obliged to avoid the shorter slalom run—used by BC Ferries—through Active Pass. They would be like a fat lady trying to shimmy into a size 6.

Even so, the circuitous route around Saturna Island is no walk in the park. With the memory of the fate of the *Exxon Valdez* alive and well, I know that the skipper of the tanker I'm watching pass hasn't had a drink for days. Even the ship's cat is dead sober when her ship plies Boundary Pass.

Aside from their proceeding on a line of total temperance, the freighters I see aren't things of beauty. They appear to have been built to take as much cargo as they can without forcing the crew to swim alongside. I can't imagine any crew member writing a *Two Years Before the Mast*, if only because there is no mast to get before. It would be futile for today's Captain Bligh to order a flogging, because the sailor would have to be tied to the revolving radar, and the lash up to thirty feet long.

Most unromantic of all is the container ship: block-long tiers of enormous boxes, bracketed by a ridiculously abbreviated bridge and a bow with no wow whatever. No barebreasted naiad guides this hulk to harbour. The container ship is so functional that the ghosts of the captains who first charted these waters—Quimper, Narvaez, Vancouver—must wince to behold this triumph of utility over mystique.

Many of these cargo carriers aren't even in shipshape condition. Their hulls make a celebration of rust. And my binoculars never catch any sign of life on deck, let alone a crew dancing the hornpipe with a rousing chorus from Gilbert and Sullivan's *HMS Pinafore*. I suspect they are huddled in a hold somewhere, plotting in which port to quit the ship in protest of working conditions.

Tugs, however, I respect. The honest tug, doing an honest day's—or night's—work, lugging a log loader several times her size, or herding scows into a docile file to the barn, is an inspiration to someone like me who enjoys watching the industry of others. Naval architects can't do much to modernize the profile of the tug, because she is all heart and never aspires to speed, yet won't back away from the largest liner, except to drag the monster to safety.

I would trust a tugboat captain with my wife.

This is more than I can say for the skippers of the glamour girls of Boundary Pass: the cruise ships. All that whiteness, and so little virginity! Like the container ships, these floating pleasure palaces have paid homage to sheer bulk.

The *Titanic* may have had her flaws—one of them rather serious—but she did make a strong statement with her four funnels. That baby was *stacked*.

In contrast, these leviathan love boats seem almost ashamed of their funnels, as though they want us to believe the ship is too elegant to have exhaust. This may be why, the one time my wife and I booked onto a cruise ship, we nearly suffocated from diesel fumes delivered by the pitiless air conditioning. The portholes don't open, you know, in these glitzy barges. So, as I sit on our cottage deck (whose air conditioning was designed by Mother Nature) and a cruise ship drifts past, I picture all the passengers dead in their gas chambers.

The Flying Dutchman with a floor show.

I'm also reminded that the poet Earle Birney, who was a frequent guest at a Bowen Island waterfront cottage, liked to write in the buff, seated in an open loft. This poetic licence added to the scenery gazed upon by the passengers of passing vessels. I have been tempted to do likewise, consorting with the Muse on our deck, starkers, in full view of *The Randy Princess*. But instinct tells me that somewhere, on a little-known page of maritime law, it is written that it is a serious offence to moon a cruise ship.

A pity, that. With so many of our coastal vistas having been scalped by clearcut logging, it would have been nice to offer a nudity that showed some signs of life.

14

The Tree That's Me

As they pass by in cruise ships, tourists can at least enjoy the sight of our conifers. I haven't counted the number of evergreens on our couple of acres, but I guess there are enough to help sustain the image of Saturna as a treed paradise.

Most of our trees are coastal pine of one kind or another. The young pine are comely, the old gaunt, or half-fallen. Many have small, vivid green candlesticks at the branch ends, as though the woods were having a birthday party. We have a lifetime supply of these perfect Christmas trees, but I have so far resisted the temptation to save $20 by chopping one down. I would sooner put the Christmas presents under the living tree, even though this meant opening them in a blizzard. We arbophiles are prone to going to extremes.

Not all cottagers share this addiction to trees. We can, in fact, be split into two adverse groups: those who have felled all the trees within striking distance of their cottage, boat, driveway or outdoor pool, and we others—the decent sort—who are willing to test our insurance policies by living right under a fifty-foot fir, and watching our gutters fill up with nut-brown needles.

In fact, nothing has tested my environmental integrity more than having a power line violate the property. If you have tears, prepare to shed them when the hydro people—heads as hard as their hats—show you how many trees must be removed at your expense, in order to spare their precious line some minor accident, like having a big cedar wipe it out.

Picky, picky, picky.

For years I resisted the ultimatum, preferring to depend upon candles and a generator which, like all generators, made combustion of gas rival the sound effects of World War II. Now, candles *are* romantic. In earlier cultures, much of the world's population explosion was facilitated by people who didn't get a good look at each other after dark, thanks to candlelight.

A wax-drabbled taper stuck in an empty wine bottle also helps to create the proper ambience for the poet dying of consumption. I've never found that it helped *my* verse, but then my problem is a minor rhinitis.

Also, candles, to be effective as a charming source of light, must be lit. I don't know how John Keats and Samuel Taylor Coleridge lit their candles or lamps, but I doubt they tried to use those fold-over paper matches. "The Eve of St. Agnes" would have been a very long night if John had. The main reason I yielded to BC Hydro to light the lamps and warm the baseboards was that if I went on depending on candles and stove I would be found frozen stiff in a dark cottage, my fingers clutching an empty packet of matches from El Diablo's.

Prometheus paid the price for pinching the secret of fire from the gods, but being chained to a rock and having a vulture scoff up my liver would be less mortifying than my flubbing the simple ignition that Humphrey Bogart always aced, first try.

But I had no trouble lighting the fire of fury in several neighbouring cottagers when the extended power line required the felling of additional trees along the road. *They* had mastered lighting matches, and they had nothing but contempt for the clod who hadn't. I knew the pariah status of a developer, that most loathsome of Earth's desecrators. I lived in fear of being set upon by David Suzuki and banned from travel in Germany, where they seem to feel very strongly about trees. For a time, my name was sawdust. I had fulfilled the first condition for becoming a hermit.

Luckily a few other cottagers along the road—equally inept with paper matches—have since availed themselves of the power line, so that we now have a fairly even balance between the Hatfields and the McCoys.

One tree that I took special pains to preserve, despite its rakish encroachment on our jakes, is our arbutus. Our sole arbutus. Our only tree that has leaves instead of needles. Glossy, go-green leaves, and a yellow bark as frivolous as a Spanish dancer's skirt. It peels, revealing a curvaceous trunk that mocks the staid form of the conifers. Our arbutus stands out like a stripper amid the Mormon Tabernacle Choir.

This tree is rarely seen in the wild on the Mainland only forty miles northeast. The southern Gulf Islands are just that shade sunnier and drier, needed to succour this exotic kin of the madrona abundant on the west coasts of California and Mexico. Just looking at our madrona makes me feel semitropical . . . sensuous . . . ready for siesta.

However, I regret to report that our slender arbutus doesn't look too robust. It seems to be saying, "*Sí*, I am vivacious, I am elegant and I am freezing my boles off."

The other tree I'm emotionally involved with is the ancient Douglas fir that stands, defiant as Horatius at the bridge, on the very brink of the cliff fronting the property. Decades of wind and wave erosion have undercut the cliff to the point where the great roots of this giant are what support the remaining verge, much as the reinforcing rods of steel furnish the intestinal fortitude of a concrete foundation.

This is not a beautiful tree. Joyce Kilmer to the contrary, almost any poem is more lovely than this tree. It is the sylvan equivalent of the old pugilist who has taken too many blows to the head and has let his body go badly, but is too stubborn to take the count.

Other trees along the cliff seem to lean away from the prevailing sou'easters that can gust to hurricane force. But not this battered old fir. It seems to lean *into* the wind. It roars, "Okay, Aeolus, gimme your best shot!"

Result: wind-shorn branches, twisted grotesques of naked limb, truncated, as warped as a politician's mind. And the topmost stub: the ideal perch for our eagle.

Here I should note that eagles have no use for deciduous trees. Leafy branches are merely impediments to the bold strokes of the eagle's six-foot wingspan, to say nothing of spoiling that peerless silhouette of bird against sky.

I am doubly glad to see the bald eagle posing atop the old fir tree because it suggests the tree isn't about to topple onto the cottage and, consequently, me. I trust that birds have acute sensory evidence of the stability of their perch. They can, I feel, detect the slightest tremor of a tree preparing to abandon the vertical. Our eagle wouldn't let me be coshed by a widow maker. I also believe in mutual funds.

On the other hand, it would be a spectacular way to go, for both the tree and me. Two specimens of old growth simultaneously felled by Time, instant quietus, and return to the bosom of Mother Earth for the nourishment of new life. Sure beats a nursing home.

Meantime, the remaining boughs of the venerable fir are green enough to indicate the sap still rises—an inspiration to my own circulatory system. Hang in there, Douglas.

15

Learning to Love Sharp Objects

The joy of chopping wood—that's the upside of downed trees. When I return to the cottage and find that a windstorm has claimed another of our sylvan host, I solace myself with the thought that I haven't lost a tree, I've gained a log. For one brief moment, I can identify with the forest industry.

The ensuing exercise—so therapeutic for both body and spirit—begins with the dissection of the corpse into butts of a length to fit into your stove or—for the nabob—the fireplace. This exhilarating task calls for a saw. A steak knife, I've found, prolongs the operation to the point where it starts to become tedious.

The purist—ever conscious of his or her duty to keep the neighbourhood noise level down—uses a handsaw to buck the log. In order to complete the job in your lifetime, however, the log needs to be of a diameter no greater than your arm. This pretty well destroys your self-image as a Paul Bunyan, despite the purchase of a red checked shirt.

For lopping larger logs, the tool of choice is, of course, the chainsaw. I own a chainsaw, and sometimes take it out of its cage to check its teeth, but I can't bring myself to pull the chain—or whatever it is that arouses the beast. I am told that it can't hurt me much, unless I put gasoline into its revolting stomach. Since I can have problems putting gas into the tank of my car—a relatively simple kind of intercourse—it is absurd even to consider giving my chainsaw a highly flammable liquid to play with.

Why then do I have a chainsaw? To create a false impression of virility? For those making inventory of my estate? ("Yes, whatever his shortcomings as a novelist, he does appear to have been a true man of the woods.")

No. I bought the chainsaw for my son, Chris, at the time he was renting the cottage. When he returned to the city, he left the chainsaw behind—a token of its sentimental value. I can understand why the parting was without tears. It is hard to become attached to something whose whole raison d'être is to massacre things. Mounted over the fireplace, it doesn't fool anyone as a trophy sawfish.

So I hire a professional tree faller to buck my prostrate trees for me. I'd prefer that he did it at night, without lights, but one can't have everything.

After the faller has driven quietly away, I lug the butts one by one to the woodpile, thereby gaining new insights into pitch. I learn to cry out with Lady Macbeth: "Who would have thought the old man to have had so much blood in him?"

It can be disconcerting to try to toss a fifty-pound length

of gummy pine onto the woodpile, only to become airborne with the butt. This sport combines all the elements of weightlifting, shot put, long jump and kinky sex that involves Krazy Glue. Because it is such strenuous activity, the cottager should never go wood-piling alone. He or she should have someone standing nearby, or at least close enough to hear a scream.

This precaution also applies to the second phase of wood-piling, namely the actual chopping of the blocks. Since it takes a couple of years for a butt to dry enough for chopping, the cottager can safely invite the uninvited guest to try his luck with the axe. Good vibes were never better than those created by blade smiting impenetrable wood.

Even a mature block can be surprisingly unreceptive to the axe. It must first be split into smaller segments with the highly theoretical assistance of an object called a maul— whose name says it all. The maul looks like an axe head without the handle. It is much heavier than it looks, and shouldn't be dropped on your foot unless you're really tired of having toes make holes in your socks.

In order to insert the maul into the block, the operator will need three hands and a sledgehammer. Trying to save money by using the back of the axe head, a large rock or your Nike walker is, in my experience, false economy. A person can pick up a previously owned sledgehammer at any local penitentiary, at reasonable cost, and enjoy the pleasure of ownership.

Once the maul has segmented the block, we enter the orgasmic phase of wood-chopping: the actual impact of axe on fibre. Nimble reflexes are required to balance the segment on the chopping block and axe it before it topples over. Some training as a headsman would be useful here, though perhaps not worth interning in Saudi Arabia.

At last, bloody but unbowed, we have the makings of that wonderful, satisfying and dependable heating unit: the woodpile. A security blanket with bark. A fragrant safety deposit box, six feet high and twenty feet long. A highly visible monolith that says, "Here lives a person who provides for Tomorrow and, if the weather holds, Next Week."

The cottager can look as slovenly and poorly put together as he likes, as long as he wears a tidy woodpile.

Should he shelter this treasure in a woodshed? Only if he owns young children who need a behaviour modifier. Today the woodshed is associated with child abuse. Why attract social workers?

Inside the cottage sits the woodpile's offspring: the woodbox. Some people, those in fancier places, insist the woodbox live outside, under the deck. Not me. I want my woodbox right next to the woodstove. If I want a touch of class, I supplement the kindling with old issues of the *Sunday Times* of London.

Here I must say something about the woodstove. Every cottage must have one, of course, regardless of whether the place is fully heated by electric baseboards, radiant heating or a regular visitor with a really warm personality. Ideally the woodstove has a smokestack. It may seem a bore, having to make a hole in the roof to accommodate fifteen feet of black pipe, but unless the rest of your decor is styled to a Kwakiutl longhouse, and you don't mind breathing smoke as long as it's nicotine-free, the stack's an artifact of life.

The larger drawback to furnishing a cottage with a good old-fashioned pot-bellied woodstove that glows cherry-red is that it will cause overheating in a building inspector, besides making your insurance premium rise like a hot-air balloon. To gain the approval of the hawkshaws, it is necessary to install a government-approved woodstove that doesn't allow heat to escape in any direction but up the chimney. I replaced my condemned old woodstove with one of these new models, natty with brass trimmings and neat little feet, and I can attest that the stove is a fireman's dream.

I can perk a pot of coffee on it in a matter of days, and the draft is cleverly designed to have several positions to deny admittance of air.

This woodstove dispenses with a grate, because the wood doesn't burn long enough to produce ash. I can burn the same piece of wood all week, just turning it from time to time to make sure it's evenly done.

However, having paid big bucks for this new, approved woodstove, I sit in front of it, close my eyes and imagine that where there's smoke there's fire.

Outdoor fires are also severely regulated on the island. We have to wait until October to incinerate the lopped limbs of trees we have lost. The Fall Burn celebrates the end of the Dry Season, regardless of whether we had one. The bonfire is repeated by cottages along the Saturna cliff, part of the fun being the chance that the Puget Islanders across the water will see the bonfires as a signal that Canada is about to attack the United States for catching our salmon in their confounded Mare Nostrum. One good international incident deserves another.

16

Elysian Fields Have Bugs

What I fear most about our cottage woodstove is that I'll find a cricket on the hearth, frozen stiff. Certainly the stove seems to attract a lot of insects who consider it to be a safe place to raise their families.

In fact, the whole cottage is a sort of demonstration lab to prove that insects are not only the most prevalent species on Earth but that they are ready to take complete control, as soon as humans get cute enough to make themselves extinct.

Living in the city, you can develop a false impression of insects as merely a nuisance, of no consequence unless you run out of windshield washer. For one thing, urban bugs are *smaller* than rural bugs. Maybe it's because the country mosquito requires a longer runway to get airborne, but it surely dwarfs the mosquito that sneaks into the bedroom of the downtown condo. *That* mosquito just whines thinly. In contrast, the Saturna mosquito comes on with the full-throated snarl of a Formula One racer revving into the Indy 500. It not only wakes you up but makes you leap behind a barrier of old tires.

I have a fly swatter hanging from a hook in the ceiling over my bed. It has swatted my face several times when I've been jerked upright by the downdraft from a hovering mosquito. By the time I've clawed the swatter off the hook, the mosquito has already made a piker of Count Dracula and flown out the window without opening it.

Also formidable is the cottage spider, which views me as an intruder. Scores of these spindly arachnids lurk in every space, including the shower. The cottage is a Web site for creeps that want to communicate. The only rent the spiders pay is the multitude of mummified bodies of their prey, littering every corner of the floor, along with the spiders' droppings, which are right up there with that of the *Enola Gay*. Spider shit cannot be removed from parquet without divine intervention. One of the reasons I hate to leave the cottage for an extended period is that I know that when I return to it, toting a carton of vacuum cleaner bags, I shall walk into a scene of insectorial genocide—piles of grey corpses and, above, the filmy hammocks of the SS *Super Spider*.

Scratch a cottager, find a char.

Now, the *outdoor* spiders, I have no quarrel with. Indeed I've never met a spider I didn't like, as long as she doesn't have her babies in my bath towel, or sport a red hourglass on her tummy. The black widow spider, which has no use for the wet and chilly Mainland, finds Saturna Island quite compatible. *Latrodectus mactans* is bad-mouthed for her poisonous bite, which may be lethal even for larger animals. In 1903 a *Latrodectus* bit a camel on the lip, and the camel died in a few hours. Having a large nose myself, I don't knowingly share the company of Saturna's black widow. One of her favourite haunts is under the bench of the outhouse, where being bitten on the lip could be a particularly déclassé way to die.

Fortunately the few islanders who have been bitten by a black widow have recovered fairly quickly, and all of us take quiet pride in the spider's patronage as further evidence of a climate that would attract camels if word got out to Arabia.

The deer tick, however, can be more of a problem. Since this bug transmits Lyme disease, it is probably unwise to invite a deer into the cottage. I once discovered a deer tick ambling across the back of my hand as I was sitting having tea in a friend's cottage. The tick was obviously scouting for a spot handy to a vein, but I hated to make a scene when not in my own place. I flicked it to the floor without comment and hoped no one had noticed that my hair had turned white.

It is therefore important for cottagers to know the correct procedure if they find a tick burrowed in the skin.

The first rule is: Don't panic.

Sadly I never get past the first rule. I panic easily, and anything I have a knack for doing, I'll stick with. But I do know it's unwise to try to withdraw the tick with tweezers, pliers or teeth. The tick will leave its mouth in the excavation, and will be more fit to spit. Nor is applying a lighted match to the tick's terminus a recommended remedy. If you put a tracer on the screams you hear, they will likely lead to your own mouth.

Can you tickle a tick? Yes, but it can be a long wait for the tick to die from laughing. A more expedient measure, in order to put the tick into reverse, is to apply turpentine or gasoline (any grade) to the tick's tush and wait for an hour. *Do not* light a cigarette to pass the time. A major explosion may discourage the tick but will also demolish your cottage.

Next, what should be your attitude toward the wasp? This is a question that all cottagers must wrestle with, regardless of the strength of their reverence for life. In my view, the wasp is one of the most difficult insects to love. Despite the fact that it lays its eggs in caterpillars, none of the wasp's lifestyle makes me really happy to meet one.

For one thing, I think Mother Nature erred in making it fatal to the bee if it leaves its stinger in me, whereas a wasp can sting me as many times as it wishes, at no cost, including parking.

This freedom to attack repeatedly is typical of the wasp's lack of social graces. When a wasp blunders into the cottage—and God knows I don't resemble a caterpillar once I've shaved—its first frenzy is to get *out* of the cottage. And what a frantic display of bumbling and buzzing that is! If I try to assist it in finding the door, does it appreciate the courtesy? Not a whit. The wasp is too busy trying to sting the windowpane into submission.

No, this is one totally hostile bug. It stops uttering threats only when it has settled unnoticed on the slice of pizza I'm about to put in my mouth. This makes the wasp the terror of the picnic. And makes me wonder about Edouard Manet's famous painting, *Luncheon on the Grass*, showing a nude model accompanied by two gentlemen in frock coats. Where's the wasp? Okay, so it's Impressionism, but why isn't the model swatting *something*? Excessive romanticism like that lulls people like me into thinking it's safe to sit on the cottage deck eating a granola bar without gloves.

Now, ants are different. Nobody minds eating an ant (a slightly tart flavour). Children and city folk sometimes ask, "How do ants always know where you will be having a picnic?" The scary answer is: *the ants are already there.* They prove that you don't have to have prognostic powers if you have enough ants. The ants are waiting, bibs around their necks and a beer on ice, no matter where in the world we open the picnic basket.

On Saturna we have all breeds of ant except the army ants of the tropical forest. Army ants would go AWOL on Saturna because discipline is lax on the whole island. Like the human population, our ants tend to be individualistic within the limits of social organization required for survival.

Our ants don't appear to get together much unless it's a special occasion that focusses on food—like the Saturna Lamb Fry. Held on each and every Canada Day, the Lamb Fry is a venerable tradition long upheld by a rugged and hospitable sheep farmer named Jim Campbell. (He was once bitten by a black widow—the spider died.) People come from all over the Pacific Northwest, mostly in watercraft that test the mooring capacity of Saturna Beach. And they are warmly welcomed by the Saturna ants, who get to run up and down some very expensive footwear and swim in wines imported in labelled bottles.

But the ants don't do much partying at our cottage. They seem to spend most of their time commuting from home to work and work to home—a welcome reminder of what I'm avoiding. As one column of ants scurries up a deck post, and another column hurries down the same post, *every descending ant pauses to butt heads with every ascending ant*. I see this as the formic equivalent of the way island drivers wave to one another in passing on the road. It is a recognition thing: yes, we both belong on this post, and if I butt a head that feels strange, I shall report it to the Islands Trust.

Given this rapport with ants, I sincerely regret my having accidentally drowned hundreds of them in our humming-bird feeder. I insist that it was formicide, not murder. The feeder hadn't attracted any hummingbirds, but the nectar I loaded it with proved irresistible to our ants. I discovered the bodies of the inebriates when I took the feeder apart to clean it. It was a ghastly scene: a sink full of ant corpses. Luckily I was able to transfer blame, and thus guilt, to the hummingbirds for ignoring a specially bought poison.

I'm more comfortable with the dragonfly, that other mis-tress of the unexpected. The dragonfly can zip backward, like the hummingbird, but has a more congenial personali-ty. Like the bumblebee, the dragonfly is an aeronautical impossibility. But the dragonfly doesn't know this. Resembling nothing more than a winged cheroot, it can fly at a pace so sedate as to defy the law of gravity, then hang a right and zoom off at speeds up to thirty-five miles per hour. Its secret: all four wings have independent suspen-sion, each powered by its own set of muscles. Boeing engi-neers can't watch a dragonfly without whimpering.

Muhammad Ali "floated like a butterfly, stung like a bee," but the dragonfly outclasses both insects when it comes to fancy wing work.

For me, however, the dragonfly is more of a benign tran-quillizer. In the quiet, warm dusk, when little else is in vis-ible motion, the dragonfly's leisurely square dance over the yard sets the tone for a rural repose. I find it hard to believe that in olden days the dragonfly was feared by peasants because of its supernatural flair for sewing a person's eyelids together. My guess is that the myth was a convenient excuse for the peasant caught napping on the job. ("I wasn't asleep, sire! A dragonfly stitched me peepers!")

Certainly, in my conversations with the so-called "darning needle," the friendly insect has evinced no interest in my eyelids. It just hovers attentively as I extol the iridescent beauty of its body. Then it goes back to patrolling the yard to munch on mosquitoes and other detriments to my enjoying the air of twilight.

As these pages are intended to be for family reading, I won't dwell on the sex life of the dragonfly, hugely fascinating, and indeed inspirational, though this is to anyone less well endowed. The male not only has two separate reproductive organs—one at the rear to produce sperm and the other amidships to transfer it during mating—but can make acrobatic love on the wing. The dragonfly can thus be on the job while at the job, which is more than can be said of most human workplaces that are outdoors.

17

Departments of the Interior

The fear that grips us all when we open up the cottage in spring is that we shall open a cupboard and find: *mouse droppings!*

Mouse turds are a strong indicator of mice. It is marginally possible that one mouse could have that many bowel movements over the winter, but the larger likelihood is that multiple rodents have moved into the place without permission.

Now, despite the disarming children's story about the country mouse and the city mouse, the fact is that the country mouse is the heavy. Urban mouse excrement may be unsightly around the microwave if you have guests, but the poop of the deer mouse can kill you, since it could host the hantavirus. Breathed in with house dust, this bug plays hob with the lungs. And of all the dispiriting ways to die, being ambushed by a mouse ranks in the top ten, at least.

However, you can also be hospitalized by your effort to get rid of this killer rodent. Unless, that is, you're prepared to transport a cat every time you go to the cottage, a taxing exercise for all concerned, since felines don't adjust as readily as dogs to being toted around in cages and projected into strange territory. The cat may just try to walk back to town, leaving the mice to enjoy a good laugh.

So I bought a mousetrap. *Two* mousetraps, actually, the second as backup in case the first mousetrap failed. Watching the movie *Apollo 13* alerts a person to the risk of technological crisis.

The initial thing to be noted about the standard utility mousetrap is that it doesn't appear to have changed in structure, appearance or lack of performance since humans first made the breakthrough from standing over the mouse hole holding a club.

We have the same little platform of coffin wood. The same warped bits of wire. The same coiled spring which, for untold numbers of people, has destroyed their dream of one day playing concert violin.

My mousetraps came with a sheet of instructions, written by a mouse and calculated to escalate a simple fracture to multiple trauma, including permanent damage to the self-esteem.

I have been told that setting a mousetrap is a snap. Indeed it is. A snap that can total several important fingers, yet leave me too mortified to go to Emergency and explain what happened. Better to live out my life as Buckled Knuckle Nicol.

I have also read a newspaper article about "the nonviolent mousetrap." The mawkish piece described the "live" mousetrap that entices the mouse into a compartment so that it may be released "out in the country somewhere unharmed." This may be why I, out in the country somewhere, have mice. They have been sprung from the "compassionate" mousetrap by some bleeding heart from town, and they have traipsed into our cottage, ravenously hungry and twice as wary as if they had led a sheltered life.

The closest thing to a compassionate mousetrap in our cottage is our stove. This is an old electric stove, possibly a veteran of one of Michael Faraday's early experiments. We bought it from some Saturna folk who already had too many suicides in the family. Its features certainly include a capacity to electrocute mice.

The stove has an oven that keeps itself clean by refusing to open the door. At least it acts like a vestal virgin with *me*. I have found the oven door open after a tradesman has been in the place. I know that its knobs have to be caressed, not twisted, for it to be turned on. But I seem to lack the touch, despite having read Casanova's *Memoirs*.

As for the stove top, this area gives new meaning to being at the mercy of the elements. Each element is having an on-again, off-again affair with its dial. The dials, in turn, seem to be engaged in a power struggle to control the digital clock. The clock is called digital because it gives us the finger if we take exception to its concept of time. In fact, this could easily be the timepiece that inspired Albert Einstein to postulate his theory of relativity.

Part of our stove's charming unpredictability must be credited to its having such a dazzling array of fuses. The stove puts the fuse in confusion. Such an extended family of amps—from mature thirties to twenty-fives and teenage fifteens—revives the excitement of changing a corroded fuse, so much more challenging than just flipping a switch.

The Saturna general store carries a good stock of these old-fashioned fuses, as well as several brands of alcoholic beverage for the cottager in recovery from an electrifying experience.

Temperamental though this old stove is, we hesitate to replace it because moving it might encourage our old fridge to fall over. Not that this fridge is easily moved. Not only does it not have wheels, but the undercarriage has bonded with the floor. I suspect that it would be easier to move the Sphinx—which in certain lights our fridge resembles—than to try to excavate this ancient pile.

Also, we have sort of got used to a fridge that knows only two temperatures: room, and that of liquid nitrogen. The entire compartment becomes the freezer from Hell. We get accustomed to chewing our milk. A steak can be left in our fridge, and often is, without our needing to fear decomposition of any kind. The fridge carries the science of cryogenics to a level that makes it a natural for space travel, if there were any chance of getting it off the ground.

The proper direction for movement of our cottage fridge is, of course, toward the appliance version of the elephants' graveyard. Our fridge is not only environment-unfriendly, but downright hostile. Its coolant is a gas that was seriously considered by Saddam Hussein as a means of ending the Gulf War in his favour.

BC Hydro offers a $50 reward for information leading to the arrest and collection of old, pollutant fridges. I doubt that they would apprehend ours, even if I gave *them* $50. Many of their old-fridge pickup crews have families, or don't know how to operate a gas mask in extreme-cold temperatures.

Why, you may ask, don't we buy a *new* stove and fridge? Answer: the logistics of delivery of major appliances to a rather remote island cottage are on a par with the Normandy landing in World War II. We are reluctant to buy a truck just to transport a new fridge and stove. And with a small car, it is more feasible for the stove or fridge to deliver the coupe.

Another little delivery problem we have—common enough for cottage owners—is water. Now, water isn't essential. If you don't *drink* water, or make coffee and tea, or wash, you can get along fine without water. In time, you will come to look more and more like a dirty cactus wearing shorts. But you probably weren't expecting company, anyway.

Regrettably I have been brainwashed by urban water boards to think of a supply of potable water as a desirable feature of our property. And one of the few faults of Saturna—and most other southern Gulf Islands—is that its water table was set for the horned toad. We have no brook, either babbling or coherent, coursing through our land.

Nor do we have a well to wish in. When your cottage is perched atop a rocky promontory, the digging of a well is a project to be entered upon with Winston Churchill's promise of "blood, sweat and tears"—each of which is as salty as the well water likely to be drawn from the grudging depths.

There are Siberian salt mines that are less profound than a well on the Gulf Islands. You can pay a well digger more than $5,000 and endure weeks of earthshaking thumps of the digging machine, only to be told it hasn't struck water, or oil, or anything but the tomb of a Chinese emperor.

You have been well and truly shafted, and the hole isn't even wide enough for you to jump in, yelling "Geronimo!"

The expense doesn't include the initial cost of hiring a dowser, or water witch. Dowsers are a bit thin on the ground on Saturna because we have so many trees from which a false prophet may be hanged. And the cost of importing a pro from one of the larger islands jacks up the overhead on the underground.

Since I have some Irish blood, for a time, I considered testing my own powers of divination, though I'm not naturally drawn to water. However, dowsing my own property, stumbling through the brush holding a Y-shaped branch in the hope that it, not I, will dip suddenly toward the ground—that takes some nerve, and no one watching. I don't trust anyone, when I'm blindfolded, to tell me I'm about to dowse myself over a cliff.

Many of us well-less ones depend on cisterns for our water supply. The system works as follows: rainwater pours off the roof to fill storage barrels, from which the water may be pumped by solar power, as long as it doesn't rain. This procedure creates a form of schizophrenia regarding the weather. The longer the spell of warm, sunny days, the less the cottager dares to draw on his cisterns for frivolous use such as bathing, cooking or—a critical decision—extinguishing a fire. If it is your mother-in-law that is ablaze . . .

At our cottage, the guest has a better chance of being put out, if on fire, because we have a 1,800-gallon water tank. Tall enough to be accessed only by ladder, the tank sits on the higher ground like a rotund monolith raised by disoriented Aztecs. We don't go as far as to sacrifice a maiden on this temple of Aqua, goddess of water. Maidens, too, are scarce on Saturna. But I do cross myself when walking past our water tank, and pray silently that the buildup of sludge in its belly isn't affecting the gravity feed or my regularity.

The water, drawn from a mountain lake cold enough to discourage swimmers who might void in it, is delivered to our tank by John Money, the island's factotum who delivers everything but babies. If John ever gets out of delivered water, our cottage will be left, literally, high and dry. We light a candle to Saint John the Baptist whenever we think of it.

Because water is so precious, you soon adjust to thinking of an Okanagan Chardonnay as a nice breakfast beverage. It can be a bit hard on the liver, this island shortage of potable water, but the body must be prepared to make a few sacrifices in the interest of mind and soul.

18

Explicit Material Online

Our cottage is plumbed for a washer and dryer. There are a couple of promising holes in the floor of the bathroom, matching the hole for the toilet that also isn't there. We have coordinated outlets. The actual appliances themselves are the only facilities lacking. One day we shall build them, and we shall come. Clean.

Meantime, we dry on the clothesline. Well, *we* don't. *Other* things we wash, we hang on it. In town our clothesline is an aberration. I suspect that our neighbours see it as a primitive structure that degrades property values. We have had our clothesline severed a couple of times by zealots whose fundamental faith in progress is based on the dryer.

Here in the outback, however, our clothesline is viewed

as a bit of an affectation. We are seen by some islanders as showing off, not only that we have more than one towel or shirt but that we make a fetish of laundry.

For that reason, we avoided erecting a clothesline that looked ostentatious. I mean, we didn't string it across the driveway as if it were a banner to welcome the queen.

Au contraire. Our clothesline is unobtrusive, or as much so as can be any outdoor demonstration of enough under-wear to advertise a slight bladder problem.

We designed our clothesline to blend with the natural ambience. No post. Our line simply demonstrates that it is the cheapest distance between two trees. This classic con-cept loses some efficacy, we found, when it crosses a main path at a height rife with unplanned decapitation. I there-fore speak from experience when I advise the taller person (over five feet) installing a clothesline to consider carefully the hard choice: a clothesline either high enough to walk under, or low enough to hang the wash on. (No fair using a box to stand on. That can be lethal when you're trying to peg a bedsheet in a high wind.)

It follows that one of the most critical calculations the cottager must make is that of the ideal height at which to screw the pulley hooks into the supporting tree trunks. Allowance must be made for clothesline sag, a common affliction that can lower a loaded clothesline by as much as twenty feet, guaranteeing a facial encounter with wet socks.

Our clothesline, I regret to say, falls into the swayback category. I rationalize the flaw by thinking of the line as part of our security system. It will snag any nighttime intruder over two feet high.

I should also warn about a problem with clothes-pegs. Perhaps influenced by seeing too many birds, clothes-pegs develop the capacity of independent movement. You find them everywhere but in the peg box where they belong. In short, clothes-pegs are flighty and have no sense of attachment.

That said, the blessings of the cottage clothesline are a boon beyond dispute:

- The clothesline is one of the earliest triumphs of solar power. It immediately identifies the owner as concerned about energy conservation. Either that, or too tight to buy a dryer. Whatever the motivation, I find it a mystery why BC Hydro doesn't supplement its bills with a brochure exhorting customers to turn in their kilowatt-gobbling dryers for one of God's own power lines.

- The clothesline serves goldfinches and other feathered treats as a rest facility. Everyone knows that it is good luck to have a bird poop on your clean shirt.

- A brisk nor'easter will blow the hell out of static cling.

- In an emergency, you can hang all your whites on the clothesline to enable the air-rescue crew to home in on your broken leg.

- Best of all, on a sunny summer day, it is a joy to lounge in the yard and, like a commodore watching a sail-past, admire your gaily bannered line—the festive array of Fruit of the Loom knickers, the trousers shrunk to shorts, the tumult of towels only slightly grubbier than before they were washed.

Better to enjoy a clothesline than never to have laved at all.

"Hold on," you say. "Where does your dirty wash water go?"

Visitors often ask me that at the cottage, especially after I've made them a cup of tea. They know we don't have a sewer or a septic tank. And they see the wash water going down the sinkhole. I can't blame them for suspecting I've set up my own system for recycling the wash water—including that from the shower stall—and pumping it back up for the coffee break.

Sometimes I let the visitor keep wondering. It depends on whether the person has dropped in uninvited and bears no resemblance whatever to Miss Universe.

However, I have felt obliged to satisfy the curiosity of the Capital Region District building inspector. This itinerant authority is empowered to withhold your occupancy permit until you've fulfilled all the requirements of the building code, including a demonstrated concern for the fate of your waste water.

Now, the occupancy permit is like a marriage certificate. Without it, you and your house are just shacked up together. You can't get divorced properly because, in the eyes of the authorities, you have never been legally wed. After a while, your cottage reflects this lack of commitment. Not only does it pass water dysfunctionally, but the windows glaze over and the illegal wiring becomes dangerously neurotic.

But I wanted a lasting relationship with my cottage. So I did the right thing. I gave it a grey-water trap. You readers who have only flirted with a cottage—renting, say—may never have even heard of a grey-water trap. But to the building inspector the trap is like a solemn vow to love, honour and drain your abode, as per regulations. All else is mere infatuation.

The code lays down very precise specifications for the grey-water trap. I immediately saw that draining the slops via hose into a plastic bucket wouldn't do. Also, the crawl space under the cottage being one of many places that activate my claustrophobia, work would be slowed by intervals of screaming. So I paid the contractor to construct our grey-water box. But I think I would recognize it if I saw it. It is much like a sandbox, though children should perhaps not be encouraged to play in it unless the TV is broken.

How does your grey water find its way to the trap? Here you must recognize the gravity of the situation. That is, unless your cottage is built on a slope, to benefit from the insistence of water to run downhill, the water may not reach your trap in your lifetime.

The lesson here: it was a mistake to build your cottage on perfectly flat land. Doing so meant that your water—grey, yellow or worse—has no place to run to. You know the feeling. Flatlanders have to buy an electric pump to get rid of just about all waste except teenage kids. And pump dependency erodes the peace of mind that should be the main benefit of the cottage after property values go down the tube.

Since our cottage teeters atop a cliff, our grey water courses smartly to the grave. How it percolates thence I know and care not, though I suspect it nourishes the wild barley grass whose hackles can pierce leather. Nobody has it all.

19

No Locks on Our Goats

How can you tell you are really free of the city?

Answer: when you feel guilty about locking your door. *Any* door. Cottage door, car door, outhouse door. Locking it, you see, is just a nasty habit.

For it is written: the chain that binds us to materialism is the key chain. The Saturna Island regulars can readily spot weekenders in from town: they jingle. When they park their cars in front of the general store, they lock them. Who do they think might steal them? The cat sunning herself on the porch?

There is very little car theft on Saturna, or on any of the other Gulf Islands, because the only way to get the vehicle off the island is by the ferry. And the chances of being greeted on arrival by a very large Mountie are slightly more than 100 percent.

In fact, you are more likely to find an *additional* car on your property, besides your own wheels, because Saturna is one of the places where old cars come to die. Unless you actively discourage your yard from becoming the Forest Lawn for clunkers, you may have to pay hundreds of dollars to have the deceased Dodge front-loadered off your land and hauled away to that Great Scrapyard in the Sky.

Still, it took me a while to overcome my urban fixation about locking my car doors even when I wasn't in the vehicle. I only recently stopped putting the Club on the steering wheel when I visit Saturna's St. Christopher's Church. That's progress.

When I take our rubbish into the island's recycling depot, I deliberately leave the windows down, and the trunk open, to impress any observer with my adaptation to trusting people.

The last major heist on Saturna occurred some years ago when a couple of optimists on a fish boat came ashore to rip off one of Jim Campbell's sheep. They must have been using some stimulant before undertaking this woolly quest, because they shot and wounded several sheep before they finally downed one and toted it aboard. Needless to say, this noisy enterprise didn't go unnoticed, with the result that the muttoneers were easily intercepted by an RCMP patrol boat and charged with unlawful possession of a dead ruminant.

For the same reason—insularity—cattle rustlers don't thrive on Saturna. Some of the small ranches at the north end of the island have a few steers grazing languidly on the lush meadows, but the owners feel no pressure to brand them. Presumably a Hereford is ferried to market from time to time. No one notices except the cow. Stampedes are extremely rare, even when the pub opens.

Persons with illicit intentions tend to avoid not only

Saturna's livestock but the island itself. There is, for instance, no camping on this island. None. Signs along the main roads make it clear that visitors are welcome as long as they keep moving at no more than twenty-five miles per hour. RVs will search in vain for parking spaces, hookups, barbie pits. Only at the provincial marine park are visitors allowed to pause briefly and use the public toilets that are hidden in the woods to discourage triflers.

Some would-be visitors try to compensate for Saturna's stony attitude toward nomads by arriving in a toilet-equipped cruiser or sailboat. These smart alecks quickly discover that the island is girted on most sides by hungry reefs ready to eat keel for lunch. Boot Cove does provide anchorage, and a marina, but only because residents have found the provincial government reluctant to let them mine the entrance.

Non-islanders who manage to make it to shore find that Saturna's main recreational facility is that of getting hopelessly lost. While all the main roads are clearly signposted, none of them gives a hint of destination. Hikers are directed to walk in circles, or over sheer cliffs. Bikers somehow find themselves toiling up 1,400-foot Mount Warburton Pike on a road whose potholes are capacious enough to swallow an army jeep.

Despite the fact that the animals create a potentially fatal—to all parties—hazard on the island's roads, there are virtually no Deer Crossing signs. It may be argued that the deer saunter across the roads for their entire length and anywhere, day or night. But the suspicion lingers that the permanent residents of Saturna, whose fenders and grilles are badly dinked, view a visitor's collision with a family of deer as nature's way of thinning the herd, whether the herd be ungulant or members of the BC Automobile Association.

The deer get somewhat better protection than the tourist because of the prevalence of No Hunting signs nailed to trees and weathered to the point of being illegible. These signs were posted decades ago by Jim Money, who combined his strong instincts as a conservationist with his hegemony of highway maintenance. The Money family owned much of the land on Saturna, so that they were in a position to prohibit just about any activity that somehow escaped the wrath of God.

To this day, and thanks to Jim, the deer and the antelope roam where never is heard a discouraging shotgun. Only in the fall do some of the owners of the Native reservation/forest come over from their village on Vancouver Island to create disillusionment in deer credulous enough to trust signs.

Never at risk, however, is Saturna's closest thing to the sacred cow.

"Did you see the wild goats?" is the question islanders put to the visitor, confident the intruder did *not* see the wild goats, and never *will* see the wild goats. I have roamed Saturna for forty years, man and older man, without ever getting a glimpse of this legendary gaggle of feral goats.

Yet it is a heartwarming story. These wild goats were originally, and once upon a time, a few domestic goats kept in a pretty pasture high atop Mount Warburton Pike. Only a few hundred yards from their pen stood the mountaintop that afforded the most magnificent view on the island: a vista of Gulf Islands for miles, an eagle's-eye panorama of inland sea, and the Olympic Mountains' snows sparkling white on the horizon.

But the goats never got to see any of that because of the accursed fence. All they could do was give milk and baa— a fitting comment on their lifestyle.

Then, one day, in a windstorm, part of the fence blew

down and the goats escaped. They clambered up through the forest, happily free, free, free! All the old survival instincts of the wild goat kicked in. These household goats became *mountain* goats, as proud and capricious a bunch of billies and nannies as ever tripped over the French Alps.

What the lion means to England—courage and indomitable pride—the goat means to Saturna: freedom to be cantankerous. I myself am a Capricorn (goat-horned, cheesed-off, butt-minded). It heartens me to believe that I share an island with this dyspeptic icon of individual freedom. And I hope one day to get close enough to the troop of wild goats to express my admiration for their splendid determination to endure without government support or special protection as an endangered species. What a role model! Canada should dump the tree-destroying beaver as symbol, and that loose-bowelled goose. Adopt the wild goat of Saturna— another resolution, I'd say, for the federal Reform Party.

20

A Fine Point

At the very tip of the skinny peninsula to which our cottage clings like a gnat on a long finger stands the East Point lighthouse. This is a serious beacon. All the heavyweight ships bound for Vancouver must corner at East Point, hanging a sharp left out of Boundary Pass and heading north to their rendezvous with dozens of docks that would be quite annoyed if they got stood up because their vessels foundered on a reef.

Now, most lighthouses are pictured on a rakish rock, with scarcely room to swing a lifeboat. If the lighthouse keeper has more than two kids, he has to drown one, because there just isn't enough space for them to play outside.

Saturna's light has none of that. The stately tower presides over several acres of grassy clifftop, a veritable golf course for the terminally weird. So majestic is this promontory that, in the summer of 1791, it was noted in the log of the Spanish explorer Captain José Maria Narvaez, who dubbed it Punta de Santa Saturnina. (I quote the brass plaque that now commemorates the historic sighting.)

Narvaez—who also lent his name to the exquisite bay visible from our cottage—must have been suitably impressed to have christened the point with the name of his ship. And he merely saw it en passant. Had he landed and walked its half-mile perimeter, as I have, he might have been tempted to stay, plant a field of Spanish onions and watch realty values zoom.

From his hacienda, he would have gazed down upon some of nature's most fantastic sculpture: sandstone carved and polished by wind and wave into shapes suggesting a Henry Moore gone madcap. This character-filled cliff face is pocked with erosions—upper-class housing for the swifts that buzz the brink. One of the larger basins served as a Jacuzzi/bathtub for the lighthouse keeper years ago. This old bachelor had observed that high tide filled the bowl of sun-warmed rock, and he had only to install a concrete drain to enjoy his private spa, content to let King Neptune serve as his bath valet.

Today the lighthouse keeper's outdoor pool is abandoned, along with the lighthouse keeper. As I write this, a war of words is still being waged between the Department of Fisheries and Oceans and us West Coasters, who fiercely object to the feds' automation of our lighthouses, including the Saturna light.

In our highly editorial opinion, the lighthouse beacon should be governed by the same rule my mother laid down for me: Do not go around in unsupervised circles. Hence our rage against the scoundrels who have cast out the keeper of the light, which now stands bleak against the sky— unmanned, unwomaned, childless and dedogged.

To me—and other sensitive beings—a lighthouse without a keeper is like a body without a soul. There may be a gleam in the eye, but where's the heart?

Surely it is better to know that the light is kept bright and burnished by a human being. And no ordinary human. The willingly marooned lighthouse keeper *has* to be someone at peace with himself and his family, since he can't jump into a car and, like Stephen Leacock's Lord Ronald in *Nonsense Novels*, drive madly off in all directions, not without severely taxing the vehicle's shocks.

The lighthouse, unique among man-made structures, stands as a good deed in a naughty world. And its living keeper radiates hope. The lighthouse keeper has to be able to hack it on his own, and be happy with the high he gets from running up and down the spiral staircase.

In Event of Fire or Other Emergency, Inform Lighthouse Keeper. That sign still comforts the walls of some cottages on Saturna, as a verbal security blanket. A person could sleep soundly, knowing the keeper was up there at the light, confidently puffing his pipe and fondling an industrial-strength fire extinguisher. Now, I feel so unkept.

As for the threatened loss of the lighthouse foghorn, as well, I'd mourn the voice of autumn. Maybe mariners have faith enough in their radar to keep them off those deadly shoals shrouded in mist, but I don't. Those little blips on a screen are readily ignored by a skipper who has been hoisting more than his anchor. But the foghorn is hard to ignore. The ear remains sober after the four other senses have passed out.

Mercifully the Saturna lighthouse grounds are currently being caretakered by an elderly island couple who provide access to the fields skirting the beacon—a glory of grasses and wildflower, where the garter snake grows fat and every prospect pleases.

Seaward, that view commonly includes a gaggle of small powerboats, idling, each with three pleasure fishermen aboard. Each trio has been drawn to the churning riptide and the reefs by their reputation for being the haunt of the enormous, contentious salmon that forced Godzilla out of Tokyo Bay, to the detriment of that city.

Long though I've watched from the bench atop the cliff, I have never seen a fisherman catch anything, except maybe a stubborn cold. No matter. These fishermen have come a considerable distance in order to cast their lines into waters reputed to be more ecstasizing than sex. They know they are matching wits with a coho or chinook or sockeye of not only prodigious weight but a wiliness that, had the fish hands to shake with, could get it elected to highest public office.

These men would be out there fishing, even though the Department of Fisheries and Oceans had confirmed, with an official announcement, that there were no salmon— none, zilch—south of the sixtieth parallel. These fishermen would sooner abandon belief in God.

They would be out there fishing in defiance of posted regulations:

- It is prohibited to use bait or lures.

- Hooks may not be placed on lines.

- No trolling, casting, spearing, netting or grabbing with bare hands.

- If a suicidal fish jumps into your boat, insist that it return to the water, using force if necessary.

I have never observed clusters of women fishing off East Point. Apparently women lack the primitive hunter/gatherer/fisher gene that drives men to spend thousands of hours and dollars trying to outwit one of the dumbest creatures on Earth. An activity that spells companionship without conversation holds no appeal for women, whether the intercourse be amatory or piscatory.

I leave the East Point Lighthouse park with spirits raised by these varied offerings of organically grown food for thought. Captain Narvaez knew a noble point when he saw one. For anyone who has experienced its beauty, dying and going to Heaven could be something of a letdown.

21

Neighbours— Who Needs Them?

Neighbours mean two different things in the city and on Saturna. Distance apart becomes relative. On the island, the nearest cottage can be a quarter mile away, but the person living in it is my neighbour. In the city, the people in the house ten feet away from ours can be just . . . the people next door.

We share the same security system. They are authorized to let the fire department or police into our house when it shrieks. It's not what you'd call a heartwarming relationship.

On Saturna I have a *neighbour*. His cottage is barely visible through the trees from our place.

On the island, the concern is that your neighbour is either your friend or, God forbid, your enemy. He cannot be indifferent. And the enmity of island neighbours is far more ferocious than that of neighbours in the city, where discharging firearms is banned. Nowhere is there clearer demonstration of that old theorem: "The enemy of my enemy is my friend."

The foe-born friendship is a staple of Gulf Islands society. Such friends may not socialize much but are found together in island committees organized to oppose something proposed by the government. The government—both provincial and federal—is responsible for more bonding among islanders, who would otherwise have nothing to do with one another, than any other social agency.

Here are a few of the things that can turn the island neighbour into an enemy, sworn if not bitter:

- *Electrification*: If you choose to empower your electric stove, by means other than a battery or generator, you must make a deal with BC Hydro. And if your unempowered neighbour views the hydro company as the Prince of Darkness, he or she will go ballistic on seeing trees felled, poles erected and cables hung along an adjacent road. The neighbour may give no sign of displeasure, aside from burning you in effigy on one of the power poles. But take it as a given: electrifying yourself can be a crash course in becoming a pariah.

- *Competition*: Good relations between islanders depend on there being only one of things, not two. Three means war. Example: the general store. On Saturna there are two stores, one general, the other of lesser rank. Still, they aren't chummy. And on other, more dangerously developed Gulf Islands, like

Salt Spring and Galiano, competition between large stores is fast becoming as savage as it is in the city. Yet they lack the police force needed to separate the combatants. The RCMP are stretched too thin to turn out for a food fight.

- *Infidelity*: On an island, the unfaithfulness of a spouse or partner is almost certain to be taken personally. The cuckold is very likely to know the person who has caused the mischief, because the permanent population is so small (350, on Saturna). In the city, where temptation runs into the tens of thousands, there is less sense of betrayal when your wife or husband is found to be sleeping with someone she or he met at a religious convention. Rush hour traffic alone is enough to make a wife take temporary leave of her senses.

But on an island like Saturna, where there is no Hilton or Four Seasons, infidelity is so flagrant that it's apt to make for neighbours who are *not speaking*. And speaking is extremely important to us. We may appear taciturn to the untrained eye, or ear, but that's because for us talking is like sexual intercourse: once we get started, there's just no stopping us without outside help. With rural people, talking is orgasmic. It may take longer to get us started, but once the words start coming, hey, get off the track!

So, having blotted my copybook by electrifying our cottage, thereby alienating a couple of my more primitive neighbours, I've taken care not to open a rival grocery store or become passion's plaything with the postmistress.

Indeed, I am on good terms, I believe, with most of our neighbours, including the nearest. I shall call him "Gary" because, coincidentally, that's his name. Gary has a key to our cottage, the supreme token of trust. Marriage means faith in another, to some extent, but an exchange of rings pales in significance beside the exchange of cottage keys. We both wept quietly the day Gary showed me where he hid a copy of his key. Its location is a secret so sacred that I would defy any inquisitor, including members of my immediate family.

Gary has a mandate to enter our cottage any time he wishes to check for squatters and other leaks. I, in turn, can go into *his* cottage if it has been struck by an asteroid, and certain other conditions.

That's neighbourliness. In the city, whom can you trust like that? Your mother, possibly, if bonded.

On the island, having a trustworthy neighbour can be a matter of life or death. Feeling free to borrow a cup of sugar is the least of the life preserver. For us whose bones aren't as pliable as formerly, there is comfort in two simple criteria: (1) if you are close enough to hear your neighbour chopping wood, he is close enough to hear you screaming for help; (2) if he continues to chop wood while you are screaming, you know your relationship isn't as positive as you thought. It may have been a mistake to throw your old empty paint cans onto his property.

Luckily Gary regards my grey hair as warranting his assistance in such little jobs as cleaning our gutters and moving heavy objects. I have to take care not to let him catch me doing something physical, such as riding my bike. It is a bit of a drag, needing to get up at five in the morning to put in a few miles in the saddle. But it is worth it, just to know I can count on a neighbour to climb my ladder and check the water tank for newts.

Yet I must not become *too* dependent on my neighbour. I

mean, I don't lumber him with my personal matters, and he responds by restraining his curiosity about them. This is the exquisite balance between good neighbours: being able to draw the line between basic life support and intrusion into intimate problems, such as marital disputes and being audited by Revenue Canada.

Such neighbours make those in the city look like inmates of a medium-security mental institution. No cottager should be without one.

22

Unhand That Tomato Plant!

Adam was the first gardener. Adam delved. Eve got him into designer apples and big trouble. Men ever since have been trying to shake off this curse by buying a summer cottage in some godforsaken place with no resemblance, as arable land, to the first Eden.

But the compulsion to have a garden remains latent in every cottager. Much as he tries to avoid seduction in the form of seed catalogues and bad company (people who smell of dolomite lime and have compost under their fingernails), he falls prey to cultivation.

Oh, at first all seems idyllic. The cottager lounges on his sundeck with his postprandial glass of plonk, admiring the array of thistles and bracken that constitute his yard. He may even show it off to visitors, calling it his *jardin sauvage.*

"Observe the bonny wild broom—*Cytisus scoparius*," I say. "Note the shade-loving salal, the ground cover that laughs at fescue—ho, ho, ho!"

The male cottager may even enjoy a year or two of this revelling in tangled undergrowth. He is temporarily restored to the freedom of man as hunter/gatherer. He sets forth to trap the wily cod, to gather the ineffable wild strawberry. He does his best to forget that early man blundered into agriculture, which meant he couldn't goof off from the family cave any time the weather looked right for spearing a woolly mammoth.

But then the old Adam catches him up. The gardener resurrects, like Frankenstein's monster.

It almost always starts with tomatoes. The otherwise sane cottager is overtaken by a compulsion to grow toms. It's as though Mr. Hunt had never discovered how to can tomatoes—whole, stewed or in any form a dedicated hunter/gatherer could expect to find at the general store.

What happens is that the cottager blunders into the local vegetable market, buys some tomatoes, discovers that tomatoes have a distinct flavour that never reaches the supermarket and tells himself, "Hey, I bet *I* can grow tomatoes like that."

As fateful statements go, that one's right up there with "The *Titanic* is unsinkable" and "Peace for our time."

The tomato plants first appear at the cottage in pots. They look harmless enough—little fronds sitting on the deck. Quiet. Don't take up much room. Or water. Thrive in the ample island sunshine. No sign of rust, blight or blotch that tomato plants are notoriously heir to in town. Success!

Then, one morning, the cottager goes out to his deck and the tomato plants have vanished. Nothing left but the lonely pots. The cottager eventually puts together the clues:

what he heard as Santa's reindeer on the roof, out of season, was actually non-Noel deer on the deck, enjoying a tasty tomato salad.

Is the cottager deterred? Does he recognize a warning from the Fates? Alas, no. He puts gates on his deck to keep the deer out. Because deer can jump a six-foot fence without even raising a sweat, the deck gates have to be high enough to add a little touch of correctional institution to the cottage ambience.

The cottager becomes somewhat neurotic about keeping the gates shut. He may post signs on the fence—Please Close the Effing Gate! And he starts getting up in the middle of the night to check on whether he remembered to close the gate himself. Worst of all, he may grow a toothbrush moustache, start wearing jackboots and require guests to pass a memory test.

Phase Two: the cottager graduates from deck pots to a garden plot. By this time, he is well into flowers as well as tomatoes. He is spreading expensive dirt where God never intended soil to be. He is so fixated on his garden plants that everything else becomes a weed. The forest's sword fern: a weed. The salal, the huckleberry bush, the wild honeysuckle—all weeds. The plant-growing mania can even cast a full-grown hemlock tree as a weed. ("Let's take it out, dear. It's robbing the fuchsias of sunlight.")

And he is watering. My God, how he is watering! He may not have enough water to feed the taps inside the cottage, but there will be water for that plantation of thirsty carrots, beans, lettuce and the experimental pawpaw tree.

The cottager has become the prisoner of his own irrigation. He dare not be absent for long in hot, dry weather, lest he lose his squash. Instead he will take compassionate leave from work. He has created a tyranny of greens.

Having thrown off the shackles of city and office, he replaces them with a garden hose—a fair replica of the serpent that queered Eden. Not pushing apples maybe, but ruining peace with parsnips.

I'm glad to say that our cottage has no garden hose. None. Somehow we have survived without this rubber coil lying in wait for me to trip over, or get fouled up in and end up looking like the older man in the *Laocoön Group*. I managed this by the simple expedient of neglecting to tell the builder to include an outside tap. No outside tap, no garden hose. No garden hose, no garden. Adam is off the hook. Free to kick back in the deck chair, sipping manna from Heaven.

This is harder to do if he has an Eve on the premises. Women seem to have a terrible compulsion—often in lieu of the sex urge—to populate the summer cottage with plants. It appears to be a need to nurture, a fearsome force few men understand, even though they may be dimly aware that homemade jungles are closing in on them in their chairs. They discover too late that spider plants have crawled into their laps and rooted themselves.

Living alone, a man can be quite content to accommodate nothing that needs water except the coffeepot. Let a woman into your cottage, however—especially one bearing a gift of prayer plant—and you have seeded the scenario of cottage horticulture. You will develop hostility toward a host of creatures—the deer, the squirrel, the raccoon, the earwig, the aphid—that you previously accepted as companions in the wild. It's a tragedy worthy of Sophocles.

Aside from frisking any female entering the cottage, possibly with a rubber plant concealed in her purse, are there any other measures the male cottager can take to avoid becoming enslaved by a thumb turned green? Mercifully yes:

- To immunize yourself from the veggie garden, you can become religiously carnivorous. There is much less temptation to raise pigs than tomatoes, or to minister to a flock of chickens. Compared to picking beans, having to slaughter a steer is a deterrent to cottage husbandry.

- Take care to compost all your kitchen scraps—fruit peel, tea bags, eggshells, et cetera. Then, when you have a heap of good, rotted soil, dump it where it will do the least good. Over a cliff is ideal.

- Blacktop the entire yard. This is a tad drastic and should be the gardening preventative of last resort. Painting the paving green helps marginally to preserve the bucolic aspect, but any sizable expanse of tarmac is apt to attract pests, such as skateboarders, or your son-in-law's RV.

What about starting a marijuana plantation, somewhere off your own property, that is? One such enterprise was recently discovered at Saturna's Environment Canada weather station. Going to pot can be a rewarding hobby, but the cottager should know: forensics can now find fingerprints on a cannabis.

23

Two-Wheeler Dealing

On Saturna, riding a pedal bike is positive identification as a weekender. Permanent residents have no use for mountain bikes, racing bikes or unicycles. Bike racks are nonexistent on the island. Welfare recipients drive trucks to pick up their cheques and wouldn't be caught dead in the saddles of vehicles bereft of internal combustion engines. (Motorbikes are tolerated in moderation.)

Old-timers watch bemused when the ferry disgorges a bike club from the city—a seasonal phenomenon, like blowflies. The invasion by dozens of helmeted masochists represents the victory of determination over common sense. Their sortie that starts out so bravely, with exhortative shouts, the gurgle of water bottles and the chemical assault of sunscreen, soon falls victim to mountain hill, blistering sun or the summer's heaviest rainfall.

The ultimate disgrace in these bike cults is to surrender to a gradient and have to walk the bike up the hill. As a fate worse than death, being mounted against one's will is trivial compared to the opposite.

The bike club that started the day as young people straggles back to the ferry dock as old folk, their faces goggled lobsters and their shorts ballasted with gravel. Although I have ridden a bike for thousands of miles in France, Italy, Britain and western Canada, I have never been able to understand this rabidity to pedal as one of a pack. To have an unobstructed view of another person's behind, mile after mile, strikes me as being a constricted view of the scenic, even if the convoy is coed.

Surely this is togetherness gone mad.

These birdlike flocks share the same plumage of sporty jerseys and spandex tights. I sense that if a biker who looked different—albino gloves, say—tried to join the flock he or she would be attacked with granola bars and forced into the ditch.

Me, I'm the Lone Ranger, riding a Silver with three speeds and a tail reflector. Biking alone on an unfrequented road is, of course, as dangerous as swimming alone, or skiing alone, or making love all by yourself. If something went wrong, you could lie there for hours before anyone came, and they wouldn't be glad to see you.

It's worth the risk, though. Biking alone, I get to sneak up on Mother Nature before she can hike her skirt and run. I get to see, hear, smell much more of her than if driving or walking.

For example, I can spot the wild turkeys, which survive on Saturna because here intelligence isn't a prerequisite.

With no major predators—such as cougars—to contend with, the wild turkey feels free to stroll along the verge of the road, as feckless as the gobbler was before it encountered Thanksgiving.

However, though the cyclist rarely has to share the island road with a motorist, a measure of alertness is recommended. Recently, on a very quiet road on the Sunshine Coast, a gentleman serenely cruising on his bike was killed when a deer suddenly darted out of the bush, with consequent collision—a rueful demise for a person seeking relief from city traffic.

For me, the biggest hazard when riding the bike is presented by the garter snake. Unlike other animals, once a snake has decided to cross the road, nothing on God's Earth can divert it from its appointment with doom. Swerving to avoid crushing a snake is, for me, the preeminent peril. This Buddhist respect for life could be fatal. To give myself an extra split second to take evasive action, I ride in the middle of the road, thereby inviting impact with a truck. The cardiovascular benefits are somewhat offset by my becoming roadkill.

My favourite ride, at East Point, is the undulant mile or so to Lighthouse Cove, which cozies into the comforting lee of the guardian light. You can enjoy it without the distraction of a ship foundering offshore.

Saturna, like other Gulf Islands, is singularly blessed with small coves such as this. The very word *cove* has the connotation of friendly harbour, of bight sized right. Smaller than a bay, less moody than a gulf, the cove curves to the human dimension.

I never saw a cove I couldn't like.

And Lighthouse Cove is perfect for the nonswimmer like me: the water is too cold for bathing. Wearing a swimsuit is mere exhibitionism. Ain't nobody here but us chicken.

No, the true delight of this cove is its beach. This shore is mercifully sandless. Sand, in my opinion, is highly over-rated as a constituent of strand. It was a source of worry to Robinson Crusoe (the scary footprint), and sand somehow always manages to find its way into the crotch of your shorts, where it can abrade your valuables.

Much more congenial, and prettier, is our cove's beach of shattered seashells. Mussels, clams, oysters—their former residences create this crunched-porcelain carpet into which your foot sinks, grateful for such a cordial reception of corn and bunion. Your bottom, too, snuggles nicely into this gravel of the gods. With my back braced by a log, I rest on a chaise longue that even Madame Pompadour might have coveted.

Compare with Vancouver beaches. There the tailored, limb-lopped logs are organized by the Parks Board. Every spring the front loaders carefully align them, equidistant and parallel to the waterline, like a platoon waiting for the order to charge admission.

Not so the logs in our cove. These logs retain their splendour as driftwood, hurled out of the sea every which way. Some are cast up with arching root systems and gain a second life as an adventure playground for kids whose imaginations have survived video games. Other logs are long enough to remind me that I'm sitting on the corpse of a forest giant that once breathed higher than the clouds.

Let sleeping logs lie—that's the Saturna beach program that suits wife Mary very well, she whose idea of a beach party is to curl up beside a warm log, sun hat over face, and snooze until wakened from a smiling dream whose details she refuses to discuss with me.

When not sitting watch for my wife, I value the cove as a resource for contact with other humans while remaining seated. Never are there hundreds of people crowding this beach, as is the case with the meat market that is a Vancouver beach in summer. In our cove, with only me and that other person who is strolling the tide line, converse is inevitable. In fact, to ignore an attractive person of the opposite sex—or even of a similar sex—would border on incivility. If the other person is accompanied by a rather large dog off the leash (as all dogs are on Saturna), it may be prudent to wait for the mutt to make the introductions.

"Oh, sorry! Did my dog jump on your face?"

"No problem! He loves running in the surf, doesn't he? How old is he?"

The social auspices are less favourable if the other person on the cove's beach is invigilating a small child, on or off the leash. As a conversation piece, the small child is badly flawed, in that its yapping cannot be silenced by simply tossing a stick far out into the water. And God knows I've tried.

An excellent excuse for shared interest is provided by the small tidal pools that punctuate the rocks girdling the cove. These freeborn aquariums abound with small creatures— baby crabs, tiny fish, barnacles brandishing tentacles—that reward patience, and absolute stillness, by resuming their normal, if furtive, activities. Ah, the courtship rites of the marine park.

"Starfish? Oh, yes, ma'am, indeed Saturna is celebrated for its starfish. You will notice the colour—purple, but of a uniquely rich shade, almost mauve. Do you come here often?"

Ignored, I can still sit enraptured by the playful antics of a pair of sea otters domiciled on a groin of rock along the shore. What a joyous couple! How beguiling the way they sport together on their waterbed of kelp, diving to scoop up toothsome sea urchins, then popping up in the elsewhere, to float on their backs as clever hands feed avid faces. I think it would be great to be reincarnated as a sea otter. All that larking about, plus a classy fur coat in the bargain! Who would complain?

Yet the cove isn't always a playland. When the nor'easter sweeps in, at the turn of the full tide, it's easy to become trapped between a literal rock and a hard place, with wild surf lashing the promontory and seawater gushing from subterranean conduits with a roar that reasserts the authority of the elements.

Exhilarating, yes, but also a show of how that charming beach of broken seashells got that way. When Mother Nature turns on the blender, everything gets the chop.

I leave the scene of tumult with renewed respect for shelter, scrambling back up the path to my bike, and I ride back to the cottage convinced that, despite the attractive features of being an otter or a whale, humans were one mammal well advised not to return to the sea.

It can get rough out there, enough to make Costco look almost like a cloister. Pedal faster!

24

The Worst Four-Letter Word

"**F**ire!" It's the cry that Gulf Islanders fear most. To be entirely surrounded by water, and still die in a raging forest fire, is an exercise in irony that none of us cares to contemplate.

Not long ago the awful word was heard in Saturna village at Lyall Harbour. Mrs. Gino Carpentier had left something on the stove while she went outside to join her husband. In seconds the old wood-frame house exploded in flames. Neighbours summoned the Saturna volunteer fire department, which arrived in time to watch helplessly as the elderly couple's homestead, with everything they owned in it, was reduced to ashes.

This tragedy—as most such on a small island like this— affected everyone. Specifically, Gino Carpentier is Saturna's sanitation department. His truck picks up cottagers' garbage weekly, on request, and totes it by ferry to Vancouver Island. It is a form of reciprocity with the Victoria government. We Saturnans depend on Gino to help sustain the illusion that we are above garbage. We have no garbage dump, and by God we are special.

So Gino's house was soon replaced by the grace of willing hands and a somewhat less motivated insurance company. But the fire was a sharp reminder to all cottagers that the Saturna Fire Department—plucky lads all, drink their bath water, et cetera—has its limitations.

On this island, every fire is a three-alarmer. That is, it is attended by the whole fire engine. A second fire engine is available at East Point eight miles away, but by the time it reached the other end of the island, it wouldn't be able to offer much except condolences.

This makes our fire engine more of a bluff—like the big "eyes" on the wings of some butterflies—to deter the fiery fates. Still, we deny that the fitness test for our volunteer firemen includes the question "How far can you spit?"

I'm ashamed to admit I haven't volunteered to be a Saturna fireman. It's not just because I wouldn't get to slide down a brass pole. As a senior, I can forgo that thrill, along with other surrogates for sex. No, I'm not a volunteer fireman because I sense that the other firemen don't need a colleague who just stands staring at the blaze and screaming, "Oh, my God, we're all going to die!"

However, I have donated modest sums regularly to the SFD's fundraising campaign to buy a fire hose to go with the engine. I think it's a shame the volunteers have to share the helmet, and if someone could develop a fire hydrant that didn't need water, I would be there, with a dog, to baptize it.

What I find remarkable, besides the willingness of some guys to combat a fire despite the lowest water pressure this side of Death Valley, is that a volunteer fire department found recruits on the island. It is against the religion of most of us cottagers to volunteer for anything. My own son, Chris, who was working on Saturna at the time of the Carpentier fire, later admitted to me that he was a member of the volunteer fire crew that rushed to deal with the hopeless case. I was shocked. I had no idea he had this secret virtue. Community spirit! He certainly didn't get it from *me*. It must have been something his mother gave him.

"I hope," I told him, "you don't expect *me* to volunteer for anything."

"No, Dad, I know you have your principles."

Indeed I do. And another of those principles is to never, never, never have flammable substances around our cottage. I mothballed my chainsaw within minutes of learning it wouldn't work without ingesting gasoline.

I regret having to park my car on the property because I know what it harbours in its gas tank—a potential inferno. The solar-powered auto can't become common too soon for me, especially since Saturna's only gas pump, down by the wharf, charges several cents more per litre for unleaded holocaust.

Meantime, I warn guests that smoking in or around the cottage carries an automatic fine of $1,000, payable to the SFD. This includes a burning gaze.

Furthermore, our cottage houses an industrial-size fire extinguisher. It is too heavy for me to lift normally, but I trust that hysteria can imbue a person with superhuman strength.

These measures are inspired by the cautionary tale told of Saturna's legendary boat builder, Dave Jack. Dave's diminutive shipyard ran its launching logs into the upper end of Boot Cove, on which was built my first cottage in 1957. A free-thinking crafter of small working boats, Dave viewed the world askance with the help of a wonky glass eye. As he told the story, in his cabin's earlier days the kitchen runoff consisted of a pipe from sink to grey-water trap outside. One day, having observed rats using the trap as a hot tub of sorts, Dave poured a liberal amount of naphtha gas into the hole, stood back and tossed matches at the trap until he was rewarded with a fiery explosion. This was followed immediately by screams from his wife, Flo, in the kitchen, where flames were leaping from sink to ceiling. At the same time, a large rat, afire, scrambled out of the hole and ran into a nearby pile of lumber, where dry leaves provided tinder for a secondary conflagration that could be seen from a considerable distance.

This, according to Dave, rid his grey-water trap of rats but put a strain on his marriage, which fortunately survived, to the relief of all us islanders for whom the couple served as a model of industrious eccentricity.

I wouldn't know naphtha gas from ordinary indigestion, but any rat accelerant whose name is known to the police will not be found in our cottage. We have an emergency propane heater, but no propane. We just sit around it and pray the emergency will go away.

Needless to say, we are in full compliance with the No Campfires signs posted along the island's roads. We do everything but frisk visitors for marshmallows when they get off the ferry. The regulation is no great sacrifice for me.

In my view, the campfire sing-along should be classed by Amnesty International as cruel and unnatural torture for anyone pressed into the pyre. Having no recollection of the lyrics of any of the campfire songs, including "O Canada,"

I sit inhaling sparks with a sick grin on my face while mouthing gibberish. Thus, for me, the ban on campfires is one of the great blessings of Saturna.

Not until the island is really soggy with autumn rains is one permitted to burn. By then the campy songbirds have flown south for the winter.

If I had my way, the campfire ban would extend to Boy Scouts. Those kids are taught to start a fire by rubbing two sticks together. Why should I let them get near *my* faggots?

Draconian measures? Perhaps. But as a dish fit for the gods, I'd sooner be served plain than toasted.

25

Eat Your Heart Out, Safeway

espite having a balmier climate than any other region of Canada, the southern Gulf Islands still must defer to Polynesia in certain respects. Abundant food, for instance. We islanders have no equivalent to the coconut palm. If we see a half-naked native swarming up a tree, we know it's in response to something stronger than coconut milk. And served at the pub.

We don't enjoy the year-round luxury of being able to step outside our *bure* to pick a pawpaw or mango, or to turf out the abundant taro. You don't see our villagers, clad in loincloths, jumping into dugout canoes to go spear the all-season swordfish, tuna or *National Geographic* photographer.

On Saturna there are no fishable rivers whatsoever, and

cannibalism has pretty well died out under the New Democrat government.

Still, we have to eat in a place of feast or famine. Only in season can we stuff ourselves with the island's super produce: cucumbers on steroids . . . Schwarzenegger squash . . . scarlet runners built like Donovan Bailey. Briefly do we depend on the Saturna truck gardener who uses a backhoe to hoist his potatoes, one at a time, out of the ground, just long enough for us to understand why the island children see nothing fanciful in the tale of Jack and the Beanstalk. They don't understand why Jack had to trade off the cow to get a bean of equal weight.

This seasonal abundance is closely related to the fact that the most important element of Saturna homesteads is the freezer. Here it is common to own a two-storey freezer, with an adjoining cabin. During a power outage, the owner's propane generator gives top priority to the freezer. Any spare power goes to the house lights, water heater, et cetera.

I'm ashamed to admit that the only freezer at our cottage is the one in the fridge—about the size of a shoebox. When visitors see me blush, it's freezer burn. I hurry to explain that we will be installing an island-standard freezer as soon as we can afford to have a flatbed semi deliver it. But we can't quell first impressions. Our freezer stamps us as vagrants.

The cottager who is more sensible about eating regularly should own a truck. I found this out soon after I bought a sports coupe. The savvy islander uses a truck to make the monthly ferry trip to the supermarket in Sidney, on Vancouver Island, and bring home enough grub to replenish the cavernous freezer. This makes the logistics of food shopping comparable to those of General Eisenhower during the Allied landings in Normandy in World War II. The grocery-laden trucks roll off the ferry in defiance of the Saturna General Store, which of necessity charges higher prices for imported produce and has to be restrained from shelling the ferry with rotten tomatoes.

It is the summer cottager, like me, who surrenders to the general store. I do so without shame. Indeed, with pride. Someone has to support the store, which the permanent residents resort to only in an emergency, such as running out of whiskey.

I consider it to be my contribution to the balance of power on the island to willingly engage in the nasal operation of paying through the nose. Besides, the rural general store has a character worthy of preservation amid the welter of megastores. It is becoming ever harder to distinguish a furniture store that sells meat from a grocery store that stocks waterbeds. But the old-time country store is general in moderation. It has no floor-covering department but offers a good selection of potato chips.

The appeal starts with the parking. In the city, the supermarket parking lot is the birthplace of anxiety. Fear of getting dinked—my car or me—drives me to find the remotest stall in the lot, far enough from the store itself to qualify as one of the city's more demanding hikes. The return with a loaded baskart makes you wonder what the hell Sisyphus was bitching about.

At our island general store, however, you don't need a homing device to relocate your vehicle. There's ample space in front of the store. You can complete your shopping on the same day. There are shade trees to keep your car from turning into a pasta oven. You avoid the wrestling match with a rack of carts, each prepared to die rather than leave its fellow tumbrels. Peace, it's wonderful.

Unhurried, I pause on the porch of the general store to

check the notice board. This collage of hand-printed miniposters is a vital part of the island's communications system.

With no local daily newspaper, here is the only classified section in service. And every ad tells a story. That double bed for sale for a song? Confirming evidence that the Bingleys, down in Boot Cove, are having marital problems. Sam Hicks is selling his chainsaw? His lumbago must be worse than he let on. Dotty, the waitress at the Wild Rose Bed and Breakfast, is in the market for "Baby crib, good condition, $10 or less"? Another failure for the diaphragm.

Granted, the personals aren't as racy as those laying rubber in the big-town classifieds. But even a general store can't be expected to fill every need.

I enter the Saturna General Store and hear another treat. No Muzak.

Why the urban supermarket feels required to administer that musical sedation, I don't know. Maybe the plangent burbling is intended to modify our shock at the prices. Whatever, the island general store assumes I am made of sterner stuff, prepared to rough it, looking at the cost per pound of plums without support from the Fallen Archers, or similar. Indeed there are Christian churches whose chaste silence is less reverential than that in which I genuflect before the altar of canned beets.

This sacramental atmosphere moves you to prepare your mind for the hard hand of Fate. Life, it tells me, isn't a bowl of cherries, not at that price. Instead I buy tins of sardines. (I hate sardines, but they keep better than steak, which has been known to cost more.) And I buy burly loaves baked by the island's totally uncompromising Haggis Farm, its no-nonsense bread guaranteed to put a lazy bowel on notice.

At our general store, the checkout lady is *the* checkout

lady. No lineup. None of that punishing wait in a queue, exposed to the covers of women's magazines displaying naked body parts that disturb your libido and awaken an appetite your tinned turkey can't possibly satisfy.

The checkout lady is also the manager, stock boy, postmistress and operator of the in-house liquor store. She wears more hats than the Empress Eugénie, and is much more convivial.

Here it should be noted that her liquor department—which is properly screened off in a distended closet—doesn't cater to the connoisseur. It's more of a spirituous emergency ward, or the static equivalent of the St. Bernards who bear lifesaving keglets of brandy to the snowbound. The main customer is the alcoholic weekender who planned badly or has fallen off his twelve steps.

In contrast, the adjoining post office (slightly smaller) is used only by the island's permanent residents. We sometime things are irrelevant. We don't have a postbox. Oh, I suppose I could rent a pigeonhole if I felt I needed another number in my life. But it would do little for my prestige on the island. The rural post office has lost much of its vitality to the hegemony of the computer. Now the islander can surf the Net for gossip instead of talking to the postmistress. Hermits cackle over their fax machines, confident they have the latest means to communicate with people who couldn't care less.

Hermetic or not, no one today needs to live in the city in order to conduct business, pipe in electronically dished gen and jollies, and lead an active, if bloodless, social life. Cottagers have this option of breathing clean air (for example, containing oxygen), avoiding communicable diseases like the flu, HIV and relatives visiting from the Old Country.

The fact that no letter carrier will ever come to our cottage eliminates a source of false hope. And false hope is what keeps an author out of the bed for at least part of the day.

Theoretically I can live at the cottage and still be on the cusp of tomorrow's mail—e-mail, f-mail and as many other varieties of alphabetical bumf as I can access by the grace of God and Bill Gates. But I'm in no hurry to get online. Why jeopardize my fantasy that many important people would love to talk to me if I were living in our time?

The ego, too, must be fed. And the provisions must be sought elsewhere than Saturna's general store.

26

You Can't Bank on It

PENDER ISLAND—A break-in at Pender Island's only bank is being called the biggest crime ever to hit the community. A thief broke into an agency of the Hongkong Bank of Canada through the wall of an adjacent store. "This is about the most major thing that has happened on Pender Island, outside a fatal car accident," said Cpl. Henry Proce.

We chuckle on Saturna when we read items like the above in the *Province*. Behind our hand, of course. No point in acting smug. But, very privately, we may be heard to murmur, "Serves 'em right for gettin' uppity."

Saturna, you see, doesn't have a bank. Our bank can't be broken into because there isn't one. This, we feel, is the perfect solution to bank robbery. *The* foolproof security system.

Ours is the only larger Gulf Island to enjoy the peace of

mind provided by having no financial institution, or its agency, or anyone that even looks like a bank manager.

We are especially blessed, in my opinion, by being free of that inhuman instrument of usury, the automatic teller machine. Perhaps I'm a tad paranoid in believing, as I do, that the ATM was contrived for the sole purpose of humiliating me in public. The monster allegedly has other uses, but these are inscrutable to a person of my years and proneness to panic.

My city-side bank, whose human tellers are gradually joining the whooping crane on the endangered list, keeps trying to assure me that its bank machine is wholly automated and can't smell fear.

I don't buy it.

I know that behind that perfidious panel sits a midget, probably chained to his stool and bearing a resemblance to Igor, Dr. Frankenstein's resident creep. When I insert my bank card into the reception slot, it's Igor who sucks it in, identifies me as the owner, cackles evilly and pushes the baleful buttons that deliberately garble my messages. The machine then tells me, and the people queued behind me, "You are being processed and your fly is open."

My card is then extruded, and the surveillance camera records my ignominious retreat, covered—a primer and two coats—with mortification.

This is why it's an epiphany for me to drive off the ferry at Saturna, take a deep breath and sigh, "Such air! No particulates! No ozone! No emissions from the Hongkong Bank of Canada!"

Oh, I know, it can't last. Someday Saturna, too, will have a large enough population to excuse the admittance of a bank, an ATM, to this otherwise tranquil sanctum. With any luck, I'll have already made my last withdrawal, from existence.

Meantime, I can only pity (tee-hee) populous Pender the Lender. I also feel sorry for Salt Spring. I'm told this big brother of the Gulf Islands now has—O miserere!—a traffic light.

This is something I never want to see.

Let me remember Salt Spring as it was in the 1930s when my parents and their teenager spent several idyllic summer holidays at that island's Crofton House, whose three red-clay tennis courts were better groomed than some of the guests. Just up the country road (no traffic lights) lay the gentleman's farm of Squire Bullock, who actually wore a stovepipe hat and whose pleasure it was to invite to his garden parties any attractive lady he met who accepted the proviso of wearing high heels and a summery frock. Her reward from the squire: the gift of a pair of earrings, which the host was said to order by the gross from the Orient. Needless to say, I was never invited.

And I never saw a traffic light on Salt Spring. Thankfully. The traffic light is how the Devil winks.

To be totally truthful—always a novelty in these recollections—Saturna does have a traffic light. One. Its redeeming feature: the light changes only a couple of times a day. It regulates the ferry wait, and most of the time the light is red. A visible caution to all: it is a mistake to leave the island. When I see the light turn green, I know I'm about to embark on the first leg of the journey back to metropolitan stress.

For better or worse, Saturna has more than one telephone. In fact, most of the cottages harbour a phone. All right, I'll blurt it out: our hut has a horn. Much as I may admire other recluses who somehow manage to live without BC Tel, I don't want to be the last to know if I've won the lottery. To avoid being accused of conspicuous consumption, I'm on a party line. In the city, the party line is understood to be what a person hears when a politician appears on television. In the country, however, it is the sensible choice for anyone wishing to combine a reduced service charge with the chance to overhear at least part of a conversation that is none of his business.

Surprisingly I have yet to hear anyone on our party line, which is a bit of a disappointment. But I guess you get what you pay for.

Anyway, it's a comfort to know that the other folks on our party line aren't getting any more calls than I am. Maybe I should find out who they are, and we could have a party.

No, nobody would come. We have in common only our contempt for Saturnans who have a *private* line and/or—gross affectation—an answering machine. Why deny yourself the excuse for never receiving any calls? These people must be masochists, unlike me, who can walk into our cottage and believe that I've just missed an important phone call from a contrite publisher, or a privy council eager to commission a monograph on that vital edifice.

As for computers, our cottage has none, so I'm not tempted to join a Net porno chat group based in Minsk. Such electronic cocooning has this hazard: what emerges from the cocoon is not a social butterfly but an evil moth, fluttering toward the firelight of Hell.

This is not to say that all Saturnans have shunned Satan's Apple. Our building contractor, Chuck Alp, now has one of these devices that work the reverse of Pandora's box: open it, and all manner of wicked things fly into it.

Chuck's excuse: his accounts had become too complex to manage for a person with only ten fingers. Thank God Chuck's computer hasn't affected his dedication to building sturdy, beautifully designed cottages at a financial loss. He can just find the bottom line more quickly and get on with the next project that will cost him more than he earns.

But I have no desire to accelerate the underestimation of my expenses. Not knowing a broadsheet from a horse blanket, I remain the apostle of paper and pencil. Forgive them, O Lord, for they know not what they dupe.

27

Beauty and the Bistro

In an African jungle, the watering hole is where tourists lodge in a tree house to observe the other wild beasts come to drink and hold rowdy parties. On Saturna Island, the watering hole is the Pub. Here the tourists are observed by the local creatures from the vantage point of the pool table.

The Pub is, at this writing, the only tavern on the island. Snugged in discreetly beside the ferry dock and beneath a convenience store, it doesn't flaunt libation. Granted, there is ample opportunity for the satisfied patron to walk off the end of the wharf, but this doesn't appear to have polluted the water around the slip. Crabs crawl and scampering schools of minnows play among the pilings. It appears that any ditched pubsters are retrieved quickly and returned to

Vancouver before they start leaking something deleterious to marine life.

The Pub's patrons may be classified thus:

- Permanent residents seeking company to ward off cabin fever, whose only cure is a brew taken internally.

- The summer cottagers—like me—who quickly tire of their own cooking and drive to the Pub for a decent meal at a very reasonable price. It's a deeply moving experience to find that there is life after McDonald's.

- The day-trippers, most of whom just want to use the Pub's loo, but feel obliged to order a Coke. It's a nuisance, but probably preferable to having them pee at large.

There's no maître d' at the Pub, and patrons are left to find their way to tables. For some visitors, this is their first taste of an unguided tour. Pure adventure, for most. For others, mostly Europeans, it's a bit scary. Tourists from Toronto have been heard to utter a muted laugh of hysteria. Only a few yield to actual panic, scuttling into the washroom and waiting there for someone to bring them a menu.

There is, of course, no printed menu at the Pub, in French or the other official language. If the patron is determined to be curious about what he or she can order, the information is readily available from the bartender. The bartender (Gloria) is in a position to know the bill of fare because she is also the chef. Further confirmation may be obtained from the waiter (Gloria) or the busperson (Gloria).

Gloria, in excelsis, exemplifies the superiority of the barmaid over the barman. As demonstrated in countless western films, the male bartender is something of a wimp, unable to control violent customers, and the first person to hit the deck when the bullets start flying. But the English barmaid—in whose mould Gloria is cast—serves as mistress of every situation, a civilizing influence, an attractive woman who remains a lady in a rugged, largely male environment.

The barmaid defines the pub. Without her we have a mere bar, a saloon, or that tacky tavern of the West Coast—a beer parlour. Yes, beer *has* been known to be served at our Pub, without the insistence of the patron. But there's little reason to treat the place as a bibulous rathskeller.

For the dining prude, the Pub does have a nonsmoking section as well as areas for smoking and chewing. I personally hesitate to ask for nonsmoking within earshot of rugged islanders sucking coffin nails at their tables. A fussy concern for longevity earns no respect here. A person worried about ambient tobacco smoke is obviously engaged in some low-risk occupation such as writing. He isn't dicing with death on a daily basis. He may even wear Calvin Klein underwear.

It follows that, had there been tobacco-smoking segregation at the Last Supper, Judas would have been sitting alone in nonsmoking. He was the only disciple trying to provide for the future, financially, in this world. Jesus, however, would have almost certainly been puffing a cigar.

That's why I never ask Gloria for the nonsmoking section. My lungs will just have to live with it.

For the Saturna visitor willing to venture beyond the publican purlieu of the wharf, the island offers that country cousin of the hotel—the bed-and-breakfast. B & Bs proliferate on the Gulf Islands, like the homely broom shrub. Residents of big old homes become aware of the blessings that extending hospitality will bring them: income-tax write-offs. They can continue to live in their roomy houses while receiving absolution for most of the expenses of running them.

All the house owner has to do is put up a sign out front reminiscent of an olde English inn—Ye Bonny Bedde & Breakfast—hang a spare copper teakettle on it and wait for the rewards from Revenue Canada.

The only drawback is actually having guests.

Somehow word gets out that the B & B is open for business, and tourists turn up, expecting to be put up for the night (bed) and fed in the morning (breakfast), regardless of whether the couple owning the place had other plans.

Posting a permanent No Vacancy sign can arouse suspicion. There are always other people on the island who get envious of anyone successful in diddling the queen's exchequer. It is necessary, therefore, that the B & B admit at least a few travellers, especially if they are an older man accompanied by a young, pregnant woman who glows in the dark.

But that means work. Serving breakfast to strangers isn't recommended as a way to help stop smoking, drinking or mainlining illegal drugs. Only the hardiest survive as B & B operators, and they must be fond of company to the point of dementia. A few of these still persist on Saturna, despite the antisocial mystique of the island. The other residents and we cottagers tolerate the implied promiscuous sociability of the B & B, as long as it doesn't get into the drinking water.

The island is, however, having a harder time adjusting to the recent opening of a gourmet restaurant in Boot Cove. I won't divulge the name of this outlandish establishment, because no one expects the place to last more than six months. Other Gulf Islands—Salt Spring, Mayne, Galiano— and certainly Vancouver Island, with its flamboyant Empress Hotel, boast restaurants that gain a rating in the glossy magazines. But Saturna has, to date, escaped recognition for anything, least of all for offering international cuisine.

The fear, among us Saturnans, is that this den of connoisseurs will attract people to the island for the sole purpose of eating.

This is how moral fibre starts to unravel: with belly worship. Eating to live, not living to eat is a credo that helps to spare the island from the excesses of the Lucullan lifestyle of the city. Gustatory ignorance, if not bliss, does help to keep food expenses down to basic baked beans and bacon, with, inalterably, french fries, anointed with the sacramental ketchup.

This doesn't mean that sins of the flesh are totally unknown on Saturna. Sexual intercourse, for instance, has been known to occur here for purposes other than reproduction or adding interest to the pelvic tilt. But the community does reduce temptation, we Saturnans believe, by not having sex education in the high school. This is made easier by the island's not having a high school. Teenage students must commute by motorboat to less fortunate islands. By the time they get home in the evening, they are ready to eat a simple meal and go to bed without a carnal thought in their heads.

Hopefully they will be mature adults before they ever have relations with a headwaiter.

28

The Cozy Cathedral

Saturna has a state religion—anglicism. It's a fitting faith in the rebellious spirit of Henry VIII and the island residents. We take no orders from Rome. Men may be divorced not only from their wives but even larger areas of influence.

This island has just one church, structurally as well as spiritually. Either you attend the weekly service at St. Christopher's, or you voyage to another island that doesn't know its own mind, or, like me, you are a devout Determinist who prays only before major surgery.

In its architecture, St. Christopher's is a hymn of praise for the A-frame. A person ignorant of the history of Saturna might assume this charming little church is an A-frame because it's Anglican, or vice (virtue?) versa. In point of fact, the island's religious denomination, and its accommodation, were determined in 1902 when the Reverend Hubert Payne arrived on the island as a missionary of his own choice.

Like so many of the renegade Brits roving the Gulf Islands in that era, Hubert was educated for a more eminent posting. A graduate of Cambridge and ordained at St. Paul's Cathedral, "Parson Payne" was introduced to Saturna by his brother Harold, buying a property near Winter Cove and thereby building a church, with the assistance of another wandering soul in search of a synagogue, Major Bradley-Dyne.

Their act of creation was that of converting an abandoned Japanese fish boat. Their church seated twenty-five persons maximum and presumably had an atmosphere that heightened the effect of homilies about Jonah in the belly of the whale.

Parson Payne dubbed his church St. Christopher's, after the patron saint of travellers. By all accounts, Payne tested his saint's patience by travelling more than was prudent in a former naval pinnace named *Gazelle*. This craft belied her name on every possible occasion and was a familiar sight for islanders: the *Gazelle* drifting helplessly on the tide, no one at the helm, and Parson Payne's head emerging from below from time to time to curse "Jerusalem!"

His St. Christopher's was never formally consecrated, and after Payne moved back to Saanich, his transfigured fish boat became a private dwelling, and later a chapel. It still stands gamely on Old Church Road as an inspiration to rotten sailors.

The present St. Christopher's, built for the purpose, stands in the cleft of two of Saturna's more travelled roads. Viewing it, you are reminded that, at life's crossroads, one way leads to Salvation, and the other to the General Store. Perdition is not an option, not if we stop at St. Christopher's, or at least slow down, and let the spirit of this gracious, airy little church, nestled among conifers, administer the message to us urbanized heathens: departure from this life is not entirely decided by BC Ferries.

St. Christopher's has no resident minister. For conducted services, the church depends on the itinerant cleric, a sometime preaching thing. It doesn't seem to miss its rectory. It hears confessions listened to by no one and exacts no penance. This greatly simplifies admission of sins.

I myself have never attended a service in St. Christopher's, being allergic to pews. Even when these are hewn of warm island wood, with nominal slivers to mortify the flesh, I balk. In the epic contest between body and soul, the body holds the hammer.

I sort of envy people who can make that weekly investment in Faith, but I hold a nonconvertible bond with Reason.

I am glad of St. Christopher's just because, like Mount Everest, *it is there.* I have no desire to attempt the spiritual ascent, but sometimes I like to sit in the church alone and listen to vespers being sung by a house sparrow in the arbutus.

Recently St. Christopher's church organ wheezed its last hallelujah. I contributed to the fund to buy a new organ, mostly in memory of Mrs. Warlow, who played the old organ for decades and helped our family when we built our first cottage in Boot Cove forty-odd years ago. Afternoon tea at the Warlows gave my family the strength to carry on. Indeed our carrying on resulted, nine months later, in the birth of my second daughter, Claire. It wasn't exactly an immaculate conception, but I do have this sense of obligation to the church that Mrs. Warlow made rich with music.

St. Christopher's also has Saturna's main library—in the basement. The selection of titles may not be Bodleian-league, but this makes it easier to choose your reading. It's reassuring to know I can browse in this library without being tempted to borrow a bestseller, or something like Madonna's *Sex,* or *Live Longer, Eat Less.*

In my opinion, the city's public libraries have become broad-minded to excess, this being reflected by the Vancouver Public Library's main branch, built in the image of Rome's Colosseum, the scene of orgies. While I don't believe the rumours about the head librarian wearing a toga and giving the thumbs-down to overdue loaners, I can value this St. Christopher's library where Christians can feel more at ease.

Cheaper parking, too. No charge at all, actually. Underground parking, nil. Uplift doesn't depend on pushing the right elevator button. For what is a man profited if he shall gain the latest Margaret Atwood novel and lose his car in P-and-pick-a-number?

Also, there's less chance of having your car stolen while you're in our island church. In town serious damage is done to the faith of churchgoers who leave the service and find that their vehicles have been totalled in a police pursuit of bandits. In the bit of roadside that serves St. Christopher's as parking space, your car may be safely left unlocked. With the engine running, if you want a really quick exit to the material world.

Nor does the minister feel obliged to take off his signet ring before shaking hands with parishioners in the vestry.

All these factors combine to make religion a more relaxed element of Saturna's spiritual life. I have seen the great stained-glass windows of Chartres cathedral, and gaped at the Swiss Guards fronting the ceiling of the Sistine Chapel, and padded barefoot through the Golden Temple of Amritsar, and tested the echo of Westminster Abbey. Very impressive all, but a tad overwhelming. And they still leave me unconvinced that God patronizes the magnificent more than a manse less ostentatious.

The wonder of creation is caught just as effectively by the unstained windows of St. Christopher's, those that frame the living portrait of the sheltering green pines and their light show of sun and shadow when the breeze stirs them to whisper hosanna.

Parson Payne would, I think, be pleased by what has become of his apostolate—a new Jerusalem with cedars of a Lebanon at peace.

29

Yoo-Hoo, 911

"**H**ow far is it from the nearest hospital?"

After the estimated cost, that's the question asked by most seniors considering buying a cottage on one of the Gulf Islands. They know that if they're smitten by a stroke, they have only three or four hours to get to Emergency before the brain says to hell with it. Location, location, location.

On the lesser islands like Saturna, the ambulance is a chopper, which lands at a helipad at Winter Cove. The helipad is right beside the picnic area of the provincial marine park. Its presence can have a chastening effect on the picnicker about to stuff his face with an artery-clogging burger and fries. I myself, sitting at one of the tables there, have suddenly lost my appetite for a sugar doughnut. The helipad greatly enhances the taste of tofu on a wafer.

However, on the brighter side of suffering cardiac arrest on the island, riding in an air ambulance is a rather spectacular way to exit, stage left. The soul is already partway to Heaven. Beelzebub will have to reach to pluck my spirit out of the sky.

The island does have a first-aid station manned by volunteers, but I would hesitate to call them for anything less than a losing encounter with a chainsaw. For help with more complex medical crises, islanders have always depended on a doctor who has retired to live on the island. This doctor has commonly lived to a great age, and no one having labour pains should expect home delivery.

In fact, the resident physician provides psychological comfort more than actual curative treatment. Just to know that he or she is on the island, to confirm that we have, indeed, died, is reassuring to people like me who have a phobia about being buried alive.

Nevertheless, I'm strongly motivated to proceed with caution in all activities other than breathing. Driving, for instance. On the island, I drive much more circumspectly than in town, where I live within easy screaming distance of a major hospital. There are stop signs at intersections of a couple of Saturna roads that may not see a vehicle for hours on end. I always stop at those signs.

I also use my turn signal when turning out of a cow path. (Who wants to get totalled by a Jersey?)

I certainly don't obey the law out of fear of Saturna's police force. The island has no police force. Nary a cop. Fuzz-free, we get only the odd surprise visit from a Mountie based on Salt Spring, and he walks off the ferry with full knowledge that his arrival has already been broadcast by jungle telegraph to every vehicle owner on the island who is driving without valid insurance. The already sparse traffic thins to a trickle of cars owned by newcomers not anarchic by nature.

In this absence of both medical and constabulary succour, prudent cottagers take extra care to avoid accidents. They remind themselves that they are no longer in the city, where they can have no hesitation about rollerblading in traffic, or jumping into the deep end of the pool, or papering the playroom.

On the island, there are different parameters of risky behaviour. Here I try to do nothing without thinking about it first, including getting out of bed. Impulsively jumping out of the sack, even if fully awake, is fraught with peril. Beds and futons vary in height. Thus, my first thought on awaking is: "Which bed am I in—my bed in town or my futon at the cottage?" Having got a satisfactory answer to this fundamental question, I turn over, with care, and go back to sleep until I'm better prepared, mentally, to analyze the whole situation.

Climbing a ladder is another, very common temptation to do something without considering the possible consequences. Men link climbing a ladder with their manhood. Long after he's unable to get a rise out of anything else, a man will erect a ladder with intent to climb it. On the island, this is a big mistake made enormous. Knowing this, I refuse to own a ladder more than four feet long. I may try to borrow an extension ladder, but I count on my neighbour being sensible enough not to lend it to me. He knows he will have to drive me to the helipad, and doesn't want blood on his truck seat.

The cottager needs to conquer his pride which, of course, goeth before a fall—commonly off the roof. He can't bring himself to simply admire the exotic water plants growing in his gutters. Instead of just changing the name of his place to something like the Hanging Gardens of Bubblegum, he climbs a ladder and—hello, dolly.

Lacking the intuitive skills of the pioneer, the cottager is likely to overcompensate for lack of experience, with measures such as:

- Putting on a hard hat before going to the outhouse.

- Not shaving. It is well known that all the early western pioneers wore massive beards and handlebar moustaches, as well as derbies, to protect the body above the neck. Women were, as a rule, excused from this facial insulation because they stayed indoors unless a beaver caught fire.

- Moving slowly, if at all. It takes a cottager a while to master the pioneer's knack of due consideration, watered by a slow spit. He or she is apt to act precipitously, with resultant hemorrhaging. The cottager may have been born without the slow-motion gene.

Because they are not to the rural manner born, most cottagers eventually accept the inevitable: a return to accommodation handy to a conventional ambulance. Call it the siren call of the city. Okay, don't call it.

However, the realistic steps of island habitation are:

1. The middle-aged couple buy an island lot to escape the rat race of the metropolis and the pressure to be multiculturally enlightened.

2. They build a basic cottage on the lot, pausing only to inhale and exclaim, "Get a load of that fresh air!"

3. They expand the cottage to accommodate adult children and grandchildren on their holidays—a selfless act that should qualify them for sainthood.

4. Deeply moved by their installing an indoor composting toilet, the couple see the cottage as their retirement home and continue to hallucinate for several years.

5. Having aged considerably as a result of family visits and property tax increases, Grandpa trips on a visiting ball bat and breaks his leg. Borne to the orthopedic ward of a city hospital, he develops enough post-op complications to weaken his faith in Scotch as an all-purpose remedy. Meanwhile, Grandma, left alone at the island cottage, starts sticking dandelions in her hair and quoting Ophelia.

6. The couple sadly sell the cottage and return to smogland, buying a condo within easy crawling distance of a CAT scan.

I'm about halfway through the above program. To postpone Stage 5 as long as possible, I try to keep visitors to a minimum, impressing on my children that this is strictly a medical precaution, and everyone is welcome provided he has no objection to a strip search for objects that Grandpa might step on, fall over or drink by mistake.

30

Be My Guest, Sometime

Saturnans aren't known for their hospitality. As the redoubt of Vancouver journalists and other blunt objects, Saturna welcomes visitors with open arms—the shotgun being the most popular.

People who make friends easily are here regarded with suspicion, as likely trying to sell something. A blind horse, probably. Saturna has only one resident realtor, tolerated because he is the soul of discretion about vending bits of paradise to persons who may turn out to be sociable. Don Piper never puts his picture on promotional material, and most of us have never seen him, or ever observed him setting out one of his For Sale signs on a property. He may be completely nocturnal. We appreciate his diffidence.

Legend has it that our lone realtor was persuaded to take an oath: never to sell a Saturna property to anyone with a lot of friends who might swarm over to the island and disturb the balance of nature, which is heavily weighted toward misanthropy.

Those of us who are cottagers reflect this attitude in how we welcome folks into our island retreat—in other words, as a last resort. We can tell when our home sweet home away from home has become *too* sweet: it attracts guests.

It is one of the wonders of extrasensory perception, the way that your friends can tell, without even seeing the place, that there's room enough to lay ten or twelve sleeping bags on the floor, like scattered dominoes, and still be able to open the front door.

No one can explain how your completing your cottage—hanging the horseshoe over the door, in fact—coincides precisely in time with your hearing from relatives in the Old Country whom you had good reason to believe were dead. The Atlantic Ocean is no problem. They have been planning their trip for years, probably from the exact moment you got the building permit.

How do you protect yourself, and your furniture—assuming, that is, you'd like to be able to use the cottage yourself for at least a few days before freeze-up?

Your strategy must start early.

Do not blab it around that you have this summer cottage. It may sound good, even pretentious, to tell people, "Well, I'm off to the cottage for the weekend." But people take notes. People are nice to you, buy you coffee, send you a classy Christmas card signed "Affectionately, Cousin Bobo. PS, will you be using the cottage in July?"

Other preventives are:

- If you *must* mention where you are holidaying, always refer to your cottage as "the shack."

- Express regret that "the shack" has turned out to be located in one of the few areas of Canada afflicted by the malaria-bearing mosquito.

- Say that you are going to "the shack" mainly to board up windows and investigate the terrible smell.

These measures will deter only a small percentage of would-be guests. Most of them will find out somehow that you own this habitable summer cottage that they are willing to share with you. What it comes down to, really, is that you have to choose: you can either have friends and family, or you can have the cottage when you want it. That's a hard choice, and one difficult to make retroactively. Most cottage owners (men, as a rule) already have family and/or friends before they build or buy the cottage. It is almost impossible to deconstruct a relationship on the grounds that the thought of your brother-in-law using your cottage privy makes you nauseous.

However, there are a few other disincentives to apply to people seeking to guest.

You can let it drop in conversation that a cougar has been sighted in the vicinity of your cottage. Actually there are no cougars, or bears, or poisonous snakes on Saturna, a deficiency that may be regretted but is not easily rectified by a person not experienced in trapping and transporting dangerous animals. In this respect, the Interior cottage owner has the advantage of possible attack by a grizzly.

Make sure your potential guest is informed about the property taxes you pay. Enclose a photocopy of the assessment with your Christmas card, with the figures highlighted in yellow.

Often the wannabe guest will fail to get the message, being totally absorbed in the fantasy that you are a giving kind of person. But on occasion he may say, "Oh, we'll be glad to pay some rent to help to defray your expenses."

Ah, but you are ready for this. You say something like, "Oh, I wouldn't think of taking your money, old cock. But if you would like to remember me in your will, it will make me feel better about your using that old woodstove in the shack."

You could also let it be dragged out of you that you fear your cottage is haunted.

"We think it may be the ghost of old Mrs. Pitts, wife of the alcoholic former owner," you could say. "She's said to have gone quite mad and died trying to eat a Swiss Army knife."

Even if the guest braves it, the creaking and shudders that are natural to any frame cottage will shorten the family's stay. One night should do it for any family with kids.

Now, if guests have somehow got into the cottage while you are there yourself, the problem becomes more technical. In other words, how do you discourage your summer guests from staying longer than you really, really hoped?

First, provide a guest bed with a mattress lumpier than a relief map of Nepal. Never mind about putting a pea under the mattress. Chances are you won't be hosting a princess. Instead, insert something under the palliasse of a size to deny sleep to a drunken logger who has lost feeling in his dorsal area—squeaky toys, a roller skate, yes, even a basketball is good. Let your imagination have fun. When your red-eyed guest comes to breakfast complaining that he found spikes under his mattress cover, you explain,

"Yes, we bought that bed from a retired Indian fakir. You may find it more comfortable to sleep in the hammock on the deck. It was salvaged from a sunken German U-boat. The holes in it could tell a story, I'll warrant."

Second, when and if the guest comes down for breakfast, explain that your doctor has put you on a low-fat, no-sugar diet of prunes and weak tea. Offer generous servings.

Third, tell your guest that you plan to spend the morning hunting for the mushrooms you will serve for lunch. Invite him or her to accompany you, since you could use some help in distinguishing the edible mushroom from the deadly poisonous variety prevalent in the local woods.

To sum up: it will not be easy, this guest-proofing your cottage. Some cottagers find it simpler just to be hospitable and let friends and family come when they want and stay as long as they wish. But this attitude will make you shunned on Saturna as a bad influence. Residents will shield their children from you when you walk by, and you may have hulks of bathroom fixtures dumped in your driveway. Your choice.

31

O Solo Mio

"Whosoever is delighted in solitude," sayeth Francis Bacon, quoting Aristotle, "is either a wild beast or a god."

Mind you, Frank was a bit of a party animal. He hung out at the royal court a lot, schmoozing with the Tudor powers that were and picking up material for his *Essays*.

I don't see Bacon getting off on Saturna's lifestyle. A certain amount of solitude goes with the territory on this island. Whether this makes us beastly, or a tad godlike, probably depends on what we're drinking.

The point Bacon was making, however, in his essay "Of Friendship," was that solitude isn't counted in numbers. "For a crowd is not company, and faces are but a gallery of pictures, and talk but a tinkling cymbal," he writes.

For those bonny mots, we salute him. I, too, am never more alone than when I am in a crowded room. Because of a mental incapacity to mingle, I become suicidally lonely at cocktail parties. Those people aren't company. So here is a scale of company, from the best down to the totally isolating:

- your cat

- your dog

- a budgie

- in-laws

- two goldfish

- wedding reception guests

- baby spiders

We who revel in the solitude provided by the island have no problem with being called antisocial. When we get tired of quoting Bacon, we go to the pub and parley with the barmaid.

Cabin fever is the medical term for the malady self-inflicted by the cottager. I have never stayed alone at our cottage long enough to contract full-blown cabin fever. A few twitches maybe, some fondling of driftwood, but nothing terminal.

True, for me it's party time when I get myself together. I'm happy to be away from the madding crowd, though I can tolerate madding in moderation.

This ambivalence came out in the way I felt about nailing the store-bought sign Private Drive to a tree at our driveway entrance. Even as I wielded the exclusionary hammer, my conscience cringed, remembering Pierre-Joseph Proudhon's terrible words: "Property is theft." A true socialist would welcome the public onto the land he had larcenously acquired. Picnickers, campers, Cuban-cigar salesmen—come in! Make yourselves at home!

In defence, Your Honour, I point out that I could have posted the even more capitalist sign No Trespassing. "O, Lord, forgive us *our* trespasses, and God help anyone who trespasses on our property" is the traditional prayer of the land owner.

On my first visit to Saturna in the 1950s, I was warned to respect the sign fronting the private road of a character whose solitude was uncompromising: Trespassers Will Be Shot.

This greeting had been crudely printed by a hand obviously reluctant to take time off from holding a rifle. I'm sure it was more effective than my sissyish Private Drive, which connotes that my driveway, like T.S. Eliot's world, ends not with a bang but a whimper.

About all our sign says, really, is "I am not dying for company." Here I echo the sentiment of my American hero, Henry David Thoreau, when he writes in *Walden*: "I never found the companion that was so companionable as solitude." Note: that doesn't rule out company entirely. It just means that, to us, nobody is quite as charming as no one.

One of the first things I did for my Saturna neighbour, Gary, was to give him a copy of *Walden*. I wanted him to have the philosophical background that protects us from the charge of being that Baconian brute—a loner. As we all know from the media, the loner is responsible for most of the major crimes of violence in North America. That's why Thoreau did time for nonpayment of taxes. We loners, to whom civil disobedience comes so naturally, have a hard job living up to Thoreau's example of *le solitaire* made noble.

"I had three chairs in my house," Thoreau writes, "one for solitude, two for friendship, three for society."

Very practical, in my view. Having only three chairs insures against being sucked into a bridge game, or hosting large family dinners, all complications dependent on sitting.

"Our life is frittered away by detail . . . . Simplify, simplify," insists Henry.

Simple comes to mind for me naturally. Being a man helps. Women seem to enjoy the detail of human relationships. They furnish their houses with more than three chairs, then invite in people to occupy them. This creates a welter of detail. Simplicity doesn't stand a chance, regardless of how frittered away their men look.

Can the simplicity of cottage life be overdone? Alas, yes. Even a man can run out of profound, Thoreau-esque thoughts, sitting in his solitude chair and skipping the details. Sooner or later—perhaps in a matter of days—he will feel the compulsion to do something.

Thoreau grew a veggie garden and got to know beans intimately. My neighbour, Gary, builds additions to his cottage, and may eventually need to be restrained.

Being short of both soil and construction skills, I write at the cottage. It is a less than totally satisfying avocation. As devotedly as I may till and mulch and weed a paragraph, I can't pluck out a ripe word and savour it for dinner. Compared to building your own hot tub, composing your own essay does nothing for the pores.

I write with an eraser-equipped Eagle Mirado (4H), but this doesn't really qualify me as working with wood. I sharpen it from time to time in a pencil sharpener whose main function is to create sawdust. Still, you couldn't call it woodcraft.

On the other hand, working with a lead pencil is closer to handicraft than using a computer. I don't have a computer because it goes against my religion. According to my faith, it is a mortal sin to depend on a machine that's smarter than I am, or that can be down faster.

I don't mean I'm totally stupid about tools. I'm just one of those digitally challenged people who can make a life's work out of changing a tap washer.

Other people are handy. Oh, how I envy them! For one thing, they save themselves enormous amounts of money. Instead of having to call in a plumber at $60 an hour as I do, the handy person walks right into the bathroom and grapples with the toilet. Sometimes this results in a flood warning having to be issued by government officials. But almost as often the handy guy emerges from the battle triumphant, his manhood verified, ready for sex with the suitably impressed wife or others in the audience.

This is why, as Bacon says, it is essential for a person to have at least one trusted friend who understands wrenches.

Bacon cites another reason: to have someone to whom one may open one's heart. I'm fortunate enough to have one such on Saturna. I lend him my ear, and he lends me his expertise in problems that involve inanimate objects such as the water heater, the woodstove and the telephone company.

Yes, solitude is tricky. I know I could never hack it full-time. For short periods, though, I think as Thoreau: "The man who goes alone can start today; but he who travels with another must wait till that other is ready."

To say nothing of the extra packing.

32

Getting It On with Eos

have never had a really passionate relationship with Eos, the Greek goddess of the dawn. In fact, I don't even remember meeting her until later in life. Certainly never as a teenager. For me, the adolescent morn began her rosy progress somewhere around 11:00 a.m., at the earliest. Before that hour I might have been up and going to school, but my eyes were still closed to any light in the eastern sky that might have intruded on my somnambulism.

At the cottage, however, Eos and I are an item.

Here, the day has an entirely different rhythm. The dawn chorus that in the city was limited to the morning newspaper thumping the front door is fully orchestrated at the cottage. At 5:00 a.m. the cock, or rooster, riseth. Or, failing fowl, the robin sounds the wakey-wakey, and soon is joined by the other avian voices glad to greet another day.

At this latitude, the dawn doesn't come up like thunder out of Bellingham 'cross the bay. Not quite. The night gives up its warm bed as reluctantly as I, who lie and watch the morning mist cling to the islands in doomed defiance of the sun. When that eminence casts its first rays upon the hill crests, I am humbled to recall that it isn't the sun that rises, but the Earth that sets in daily obeisance to that magisterial star, dragging our moon into lunar limbo.

In town Eos coughs her way through smog. She is cursed by morning commuters, clapping down the sun visor the better to squint in pursuit of frustration. Then she vanishes into the forenoon—the goddess that left town.

But at the cottage her summons can't be ignored. I am up and well into my granola while the TV still slumbers under its test pattern. It is too early for the news to collect its disasters. The only eye-in-the-sky is that of hovering eagle. I can lean back with my second cuppa and concentrate on the current events of the sea. Nothing new, in depth.

Then, by land, come Buck, Doe and Fawn, our visiting family of deer. In line, more or less, on the path they have made, in the course of these matinal tours, they graze with the watchful assurance of the incomparably fleet of hoof. Buck leads the stroll. He uses both ends of his body to monitor the situation. Eye, ear and nose are ample to register any anomaly ahead. The twitchy tail transmits a message that only his family retinue can read. I just wish I had something like it to discharge nervous energy.

Here is one of the most vulnerable creatures on the planet. Yet, far from being an endangered species, the deer of North America abound and are, in fact, considered to be something of a pest. By sheer flair for being prolific, and speed with which to get the hell out of trouble, the deer proves that the meek may indeed inherit the Earth, as long as they stay off the freeway.

By noon the deer have retired to shadier bowers, and predators declare an armistice. Robins, chickadees and towhees hunker down to conserve energy in the heat of the day. Even the more sensible insects take a break from flight. Only humans, the cottagers, barge about in the noonday sun, having found this the way to bake and shed their skins more painfully than nature intended.

Not me, though. I have gracefully accepted the siesta—the best thing to come out of Mexico, the taco notwithstanding.

What bliss to sit in the umbrage of the deck, to watch the sea sport its sparkle, to smell the earth respond to the sun's warmth, to hear only the popping seed pods of the wild broom in labour! For this magical moment, I am free from my shadow, that tiresome mimic. I sit in bold relief.

With this whole little world snoozing, now is the time for the writer to profit from absence of distraction, to give his mind free rein to carpe diem and run down those great thoughts . . .

Zzzz.

Okay, so I dozed off. It's noon's anaesthetic. Heavier than air at dawn or dusk. Weighs on the eyelids. Gets lodged in the postnasal area to produce something easily mistaken for a snore . . .

The day mellows into twilight, the sun forsakes the forest, the sea plumbs deeper shades of blue and the critturs sally out for supper. Our deer reappear briefly to check that the cottage is still under the same management. I have looked up from my book to see Buck gazing at me through the window. He knows I am harmless, unlikely to hunt for much except my glasses. But a different occupant might be a menace, looking for food elsewhere than in the fridge.

In town the daylight dies unmourned. Some, in fact, are happy to see it go. Nightclub owners, hookers, teenagers hot to trot—these welcome the dark to shroud the passing of innocence. But at the cottage the day is so much with me that I feel its demise as part of my own. I know that I am one precious day older, a tragedy to weep on, whereas my city days fly past unheeded until suddenly I'm dead.

Wasn't it Albert Einstein who proved that time is relative, dependent on where a person is making the measurement of moments? The cottage confirms his theory. Here speed of life is such that the traveller returns younger than when he set forth. He has stopped shaving, his eyes are clear and his cheeks glow like a child's.

Early to bed. At the cottage, darkness dictates accelerated retirement to the sack. Nothing in the night, beyond the puny illumination within your walls, encourages defiance of the dark. Eight o'clock is prime time, not for TV but for shut-eye. How many times do you want to have to plod to the outhouse, barely beamed up to that satellite by flashlight and fear of goblins? Once, I suggest, is quite enough.

I get one last volant visitor—a glimpse, merely, so swift and erratic is his flight. Some people are spooked by this apparition of the bat, perhaps because they have watched too many Dracula films. And, yes, it *is* hard to chat up a bat. I have barely time to say, "Nighty-night, Count!" before he's past. Besides, I don't speak Transylvanian. But I don't feel compelled to go to bed wearing a lei of garlic bulbs. *Au contraire*, I have nothing but admiration for the flying mouse, knowing that his tummy is full of mosquitoes that had their eye on my nose.

Now the cottager is cozied under the covers—to be

thoroughly humbled by the night sky, the panoply of the firmament that in the city is adulterated by street lamps, home-security lights and the rest of the contributors to that eerie glow that hovers over every town like a mushroom cloud redolent of the nuclear.

Here, however, the universe becomes apparent, indeed enthralling. I am cast back into the state of wonder common to the ancient Egyptian trying to form meaningful shapes from the myriad stars, and am the more subdued because I, relatively modern man, know that the countless host that I can see is but the margin of infinity.

This spectacle is not profound enough to convert me to reading the scripture of Your Daily Horoscope. But I see evidence enough that God, if any, is Our Father, because only a guy would make so much stuff with no conceivable purpose. The Big Bang was a typically male project. What I am gazing at is the damnedest fireworks display ever to linger in the sky for our oohs and ahs.

Sometimes I wake during the night, murmur hello to a convivial planet and wonder briefly how many other cottagers, whirling around other stars in creation's violent waltz of the worlds, are thinking of *me*. Probably millions. It's a comforting thought with which to conclude another spectacularly uneventful day at the cottage.

33

Whither Our Walden?

I s the summer cottage on the endangered list of abodes? Will it be overwhelmed by Progress, that worst type of pollution?

The seasonal residence has been around for a long time. Even Neanderthals had summer caves, and winter caves that were easier to heat. I know this because I have met some of them on the ferry.

In his essay "Of Building," Francis Bacon strikes a familiar chord when he quotes Pompey as questioning Lucullus about his personal choice of houses: "Surely an excellent place for summer, but how do you do in winter?"

To which Lucullus replies: "Why, do you not think me as wise as some fowl are, that ever change their abode towards the winter?"

In line with Lucullus's reasoning, most Saturna summer cottagers show that they are at least as smart as the Canada goose. They get the hell out at first frost.

But our seasonal migration becomes ever more pricey luxury—one that younger couples can't afford unless they buy their waterfront properties somewhere on the Bering Sea, and work out holiday arrangements with polar bears.

For most Canadian snowbirds, it is cheaper to fly to Arizona or Hawaii for a week or so in the winter, and spend summer holidays hiking or biking through sunnier parts of the province to acquire the tan that identifies fortune's darling. What they lose by way of dysentery they gain in not having to pay double property taxes.

This cost factor reflects a geological disaster: they are not making any more land.

In fact, global warming menaces us with oceans risen to erase much of the seashore we thought we had. Many summer cottagers with waterfront property may be fated to wear snorkel gear to go downstairs.

We, in our cottage, shouldn't be directly affected, being atop a 100-foot cliff. But seeing other cottagers drift past on the tide, clinging desperately to deadheads, will likely spoil our sea view.

Meantime, rising much faster than the ocean are the costs of maintaining a summer cottage. The greenhouse effect can't be blamed for the erosion of our bank account, especially by taxes. To explain this phenomenon, I have made an in-depth study of what causes higher taxes.

It's Progress.

Yes, I know people had to pay taxes back in feudal times before they suffered Progress. But today Progress and taxes are intimately connected.

Take schools, for example. Take them—as comedian

Henny Youngman would say—someplace else. Schools and Progress are closely linked in the myth of Western civilization. If we hadn't been brainwashed—mostly by teachers—into believing that formal education is somehow instructive, our taxes would be a fraction of what they are today, and parents would be free to teach their children that Progress is the pits.

Luckily, on Saturna, we have a wee one-room school that keeps education from getting out of hand. The islanders hold costs down by reproducing very slowly, if at all. But on other Gulf Islands, population is exploding, with higher school, road and other taxes making Eden unaffordable for refugees from Progress.

And there are sewers, too—the bad breath of Progress. I know the sewers of Paris have pretty well paid for themselves, as a tourist attraction and with royalties from *Les Misérables*. But on Saturna a sewer is apt to be less romantic, and therefore just another drain on the pocketbook.

As are water mains. For the cottage, the ideal source of drinking water is a brook—babbling, preferably, but an option only. The Gulf Islands are weak on creek, so that Progress puts their lakes in peril. As more water mains go in, the lakes will go down until the lakefront cottager is looking at Walden Mud.

And, of course, Progress produces more motor traffic. The additional people want more roads for their vehicles to get from their headaches to real migraines. It is the first thing they demand after buying their nice, quiet pieces of property out of the city: "Give me a road. No, make that a highway. The guy next door has a truck. We may need four lanes. Make it six . . ."

Saturna has managed to confine road Progress mostly to filling the potholes in the existing shunpikes. Where there has been a twenty-foot washout, they put in a speed-bump sign. We cottagers understand what it means, and visitors learn fast.

On my latest visit to Saturna, I was disturbed to see that Progress had painted a yellow line down the middle of East Point Road, our main drag. It was a wavy line, obviously painted under duress, but it still represented an attempt to segregate traffic—regimentation all too typical of Progress. I tried to ignore it by driving down the middle of the road as is my wont, but found it impossible to ignore the evil omen.

More positively Saturna continues to present a deterrent to Progress by having no auto service station. There is just one unmanned pump down by the wharf. This means that every breakdown or accident looms as a major catastrophe, that of the vehicle's having to be towed, by ferry, to Vancouver Island. Courtesy car? In your dreams, stranger.

Finally Progress is death on forests. For some reason, we Canadians ignore what the ancient Greeks did to *their* lovely isles in the Aegean, namely deforested the lot. They learned their lively dance on very hot rocks. Our forest practices promise the same reduction of old-growth forest to the single, solitary tree, which looks good in a painting silhouetted against the sunset. But the lone pine has a short life span. These trees, like most people, need company. Collectively they can break the wind; individually the gale prevails.

For these eminently incontestable reasons, Progress must be stopped, if not on the Mainland—which, according to most projections, is doomed—then on these islands. And if not on other islands, then on Saturna. To quote Winston Churchill: "Very well, then, alone." Therefore, I present my program.

First, discourage immigration to the island. (The ferry

service is doing its part in this campaign, but we can't count on its not improving.) At minimum, Saturna should set up its own Customs at the ferry dock, denying entry to baggage accompanied by people.

Second, advise all prospective newcomers that the island has had close ties with the leper colony on nearby D'Arcy Island. Plant the story that there has been a government cover-up on the number of lepers who escaped the colony, paddling to Saturna and blending with residents who had lost fingers and toes as part-time loggers.

Third, hold an island referendum on sovereignty. A last resort, this, but the only one guaranteed to get the attention of senior governments.

Granted, it won't be easy to put a condom on an entire island. But promiscuous relations with the noninsular can only lead to a socially transmitted disease—growth.

It may be that growth *can't* be stopped. But perhaps we can slow it down long enough for the rest of Canada—hell, the world—to realize that Progress sucks.

Should we try to turn back the clock? When it's a cuck-oo clock, believe it.